NARCISSISTIC ABUSE AND TRAUMA RECOVERY

10 STEPS TO HEALING FROM MASKED ABUSE

ABBY B HUDSON

© **Copyright Abby B Hudson 2021 - All rights reserved.**

The content contained within this book may not be reproduced, duplicated, or transmitted without direct written permission from the author or the publisher.

Under no circumstances will any blame or legal responsibility be held against the publisher, or author, for any damages, reparation, or monetary loss due to the information contained within this book. Either directly or indirectly. You are responsible for your own choices, actions, and results.

Legal Notice:

This book is copyright protected. This book is only for personal use. You cannot amend, distribute, sell, use, quote, or paraphrase any part, or the content within this book, without the consent of the author or publisher.

Disclaimer Notice:

Please note the information contained within this document is for educational and entertainment purposes only. All effort has been executed to present accurate, up-to-date, and reliable, complete information. No warranties of any kind are declared or implied. Readers acknowledge that the author is not engaging in the rendering of legal, financial, medical, or professional advice. The content within this book has been derived from various sources. Please consult a licensed professional before attempting any techniques outlined in this book.

By reading this document, the reader agrees that under no circumstances is the author responsible for any losses, direct or indirect, which are incurred as a result of the use of the information contained within this document, including, but not limited to, — errors, omissions, or inaccuracies.

CONTENTS

Introduction   7

1. Understanding a Narcissist   19
2. Dealing with a Narcissist   55
3. Narcissistic Abuse Syndrome   79
4. Long-Term Effects of Narcissistic Abuse   109
5. Handling Narcissistic Abuse   129
6. 10 Steps to Recovery   151

Conclusion   167
Leave a 1-Click Review!!!!   171
References   173

JUST FOR YOU

A FREE Gift to my Readers

The Daily checklist and 31-day Challenge to help get you back on track.

Just visit this Link.

www.abbybhudson.com

"The lion is most handsome when looking for food."

— RUMI

INTRODUCTION

He was kind until he became cruel. He was loving until he wasn't. Honest when he wasn't. Once upon a time, his fondness of you eclipsed his want for everything. He would trace the outline of your lips and frame your cheeks in his hands, his eyes glowing with wonder and happiness so profound that it robbed you of breath. Your love story began with a word, a stolen kiss, and a smile. His words were the balm to your soul and your words to his.

He revealed to you the story of his betrayal by another, weaving a sad story about how his trust was shattered. He laments his blind loyalty and smiles sadly when you offer him sympathy. Your compassion, he says, makes him feel things he hasn't felt before. He tells you that you ease the ache in his heart and soul, and you fall for it hook, line, and sinker.

You become infatuated with him, his body, his words, his charisma, and his gloriously innocent and broken façade. You start to spend so much time with him that you began to lose touch with your friends and family. You think to call them a few times, but he sweeps you away, demanding your attention, which you give because you love the shared laughter and secret smiles he gives you when no one is looking. In fact, he even encourages this isolation because he wants you all to himself. You think he has made you into the center of his world, but you have no idea about the predator in your den, much like prey. You are happy until you aren't.

Then comes his voice, void of inflection, telling you to do or say something that you thought was anathema to his character. You try to rationalize his actions or words, hoping that it was all a misunderstanding. You think it's a dream, a one-off incident, but it isn't. The mask has slipped, you realize, and heaven has become hell.

Torments walk into your life. He begins to twist and turn your strengths into flaws, your compassion into contemptuous naiveté, your understanding into close-mindedness, and your self-confidence into doubt. He erodes your self-esteem, your self-respect, and your sense of self by blaming you for everything that happens. His weaknesses become your faults; he rents and twists words and makes them into abominations in order to fling them at you. He keeps you blindsided and tottering on your feet, unaware of the war he is waging against you. He is a predator, and you are his prey.

You try hard to make your relationship work. You bend over backward for him, you cut yourself off from your family and friends in order to soothe him, yet he still doesn't give you back what you had in those first few weeks or months of your relationship. He makes snide and cruel remarks on your body, your mindset, actions, past, and anything he gets a hold of that is related to you in any way. He is condescending, harsh, and aggressive towards you. Every word out of his mouth becomes a power play. Every compliment is veiled in savage contempt and attacks at your sense of self. He rips you apart, piece by piece, telling you that his version is the right one, that you have been mistaken all your life.

You believe him. After all, he made you feel beautiful and lovely and wild. He drenched you in happiness and gave you peace. How could he not be right? He is gentle when he wants you to do something for him, and you crave that attention like an addict. You want to be held, to be loved, even if it is false because you have nothing and no one else to give you that happiness. You think that the highs are worth the lows. That the torture is worth the joy, you get from him. He is a drug, and you are an addict.

As he lavishes on your need for approval, a scrap of kindness, he also maims you and picks at your wounds, salivating at the pain you're going through, all for him. You, once enamored of him for his loving support and understanding, are now riveted by his need to expel his terrors and his wants on you. You are blind to his faults and slave to his pleasure until you finally aren't. His antics are like lightning, one moment visible and then gone the next. You feel the lightning strike you and realize the depth of your error, and just a moment later, you're being showered with love and affection and cannot fathom why you thought what you did.

Many people who have been through such a relationship recognize how hard it is to get out of it. Your acquaintances tell you that your partner is so brilliant and kind and helpful—so full of goodwill. Your memories of him also suggest the same. You think that he can be incredibly kind, even if he's cruel most of the time. You feel that he loves you immensely, even when he demeans you, hates you, and puts you down savagely for anything you do. He battles with your sense of self, trying his hardest to break you down, and is not even satisfied when you do break down, begging for his affections. You think the world of him, and he believes that the dirt under his foot is purer than you. He fights like a soldier in a war for total control over you, and you fight him for his presumption.

A narcissist is not like a warrior, he isn't direct, and he isn't honest about his actions. He is deceptive, a liar, callous and shrewd, and a mind-killer. He tries his hardest to destroy those he comes into contact with him, doing everything possible to make them subservient to him. He is like an addict who needs his daily shot of poison—an addict who makes others victims of his hunger for dominance. He thinks of love as dominance when it is actually the active caring and concern for the health and well-being of another person's body and heart, all the things he doesn't care a whit about.

Just like a soldier in a war, someone who goes through a narcissistic relationship suffers and gets wounded—both physically and psychologically. They cannot describe what has been done to them. They are betrayed at every turn by those they love, even made to feel guilty for standing up for themselves. They try to describe the harm that has been done to them but is often considered crazy, paranoid, petty, or even needy. When someone does believe you, their complaints run into a wall of charisma and kindness exhibited by your abuser, which makes you seem crazy and unstable in turn. They come out looking squeaky clean, but you seem blighted and out of sorts.

By the time you realize that you're actually in a toxic relationship with a narcissist, you're too devastated, too broken to pick yourself up. The abuse you have gone through has scarred you in so many ways—both seen and unseen. You believe that, at one point, you may have been the problem in the relationship, that you may have been the cause of the abuser's behavior towards you. The web of lies the narcissist has spun around you refuses to let you go, making you spiral deep in an unemotional abyss where you, at least, find solitude for a time. But, it is a solitude, a peace that doesn't last. It is as fleeting as youth and as unstable. Suffering returns, and we become its victim again and again.

I, too, once thought something was wrong with me as countless others who suffered through life with a narcissist did. That all those instances of cutting remarks, sarcastic attacks, out-of-control behaviors, cruelty, and sadistic pleasure were imaginary and my fault. That the one I loved was right, and that I was the naïve one, the one who was a bad influence. I almost lost something incredibly precious to me because of my blindness to my partner's game. Therefore, in this book, I will tell you my journey, where appropriate, about my life as a victim life as a freed person. I will tell you how you can relieve yourself of pain and how you can build yourself back up.

Together, we will go over the fact that your abuser chose you and specifically targeted you. They tricked you, told lies to you, played games with you, and tormented you with full knowledge of their actions, which is why they're culpable of them. Entertaining pity for the abuser will do nothing but chain you further to them because pity gives way to excuses, and excuses soften the heart of everybody. Therefore, in this case, compassion is a double-edged sword. Abusers count on never being called out for their behavior—they think they have everybody fooled—so if you feel pity for them, you will only help them hide their actions. Thus, in this book, we will talk about the responsibility your abuser holds for his actions and why you *should* hold them responsible.

They're very few therapeutic avenues of support available to victims of abuse who want to sort through their pain. Usually, people have no idea when abuse is taking place beneath their noses because it is being done by people who they assume would never hurt anybody. The concealed nature of narcissistic abuse is the reason why its targets are left so devastated. They have no one to talk to them and no one who believes them, especially when they're unsure of themselves. This is why the effects of this abuse are so harmful. They rend a person apart. To this effect, I will offer resources that could help you recover the stability you had before your life became a train wreck.

In this book, I will also explore the ways narcissistic people manipulate their victims, create doubts in their minds, and cut out their self-esteem until they're shells of themselves. I'll show how the mind of a narcissist works, and the techniques they use on their victims, and how to identify one. As a person who has lived over a decade with a narcissist, I will explain the effects of living in a toxic relationship with a narcissist and will offer practical ways, backed by clinical and scientific research and personal experience, that could help you heal and lead a normal life.

Whether your abuse may have taken place in a romantic relationship, within a friend group, at work, or in your family, know that all survivors go through the same steps (that vary in order from person to person) when healing from toxic encounters with narcissists. I will introduce ten steps that can be used to heal and recover from narcissistic abuse, all of which apply to everyone, no matter the location of the abuse. The first of these steps is to recognize that you are telling the truth. If we do not acknowledge that something exists, we cannot heal from the effects of it at all. Admitting that you've been the victim of an abusive relationship is a challenging process because there are no visible hurts on you. You don't have a split lip, a bruised eye, or broken bones, but the injuries you do have are deeply hidden. Coming to a complete understanding of what they did to you will help you understand how to stay away from other narcissistic people and the red flags they wave. Successive steps deal with the emotional impacts of your abuse and the ways you can deal with them.

Therefore, while you and I are on this journey, I will share information and concepts that could help you build a better version of yourself. This information will help you explore connections between what you may be experiencing and what others have walked through. These connections will help you discover the truth of your experience and the truths hidden by your abuser. Together, we will take an honest look at the effects of the abuse and the stages of recovery. We will talk about all the messy aspects of the relationship you had with them with utmost respect and gentleness. That is my promise to you.

Thus, in *Narcissistic Abuse and Trauma,* you will discover:

- 10 recovery steps to get you through a **successful healing process**.
- Ways to understand what is truly going on in the **mind of a narcissist** and why what they put you through is not your fault.
- The **harmful effects** of the abuse that may linger on you and your children, and why it is urgent that you take action now.
- All the attitudes, decisions, and steps to **dealing with a narcissist**, especially when you can't or don't want to cut them out of your life.
- The extent that the harm of **narcissistic abuse syndrome** can affect you and practical ways to stop it and overcome it.
- How to **win your life back**, regain your self-worth, and thrive anew.

And *much more.*

So, if you have picked this book wondering what in the world happened to you in your relationship, know that you are not alone on this journey. The lives of too many people have been destroyed by psychological abuse. Too many have gone toe-to-toe with toxic people and lost. The majority of those who have been abused believe that they will never get better—they have no hope that they will *ever* be better. They feel that they have no energy, joy, and no life inside them. They are weary of life; their bones ache, and they are gloomy all the time. But their life doesn't end there. It shouldn't end there, no matter what they believe. There *is* life after an abuser, and only by taking the first step does it come within your reach.

Be real. Cry. Or not cry if you don't want to. That's all okay. If you feel that you're stuck in a vortex of self-deception, pain, and hopelessness—a storm of volatile emotion—find a quiet and serene spot and let your pain go. Be honest with yourself and your pain. Find help and those who have been in the same boat as you once and are still rocking. Remember that there is always hope at the end of the tunnel, you just have to see it for yourself to believe it.

No one book, essay, or blog post will ever help you reach your destination single-handedly. Rather, your determination, combined with the advice from the book, article, or blog post, will help you cross that boundary. If you choose this book as your friend and your advisor, remember that I'm rooting for you. I am honored at the trust you have placed in my words and my advice, and I hope with all my heart that the words I've penned on these pages help you as much as they did me in the darkest times of my life.

For in the darkness shines light. Since I've been through both, I can definitely tell you that light is vastly preferable to darkness.

Darkness is mystique, but the light is life, and we can't live without it. Therefore, be strong, like I once wasn't, slip your hand in mine and take the first step on your journey. You will not regret it.

1

UNDERSTANDING A NARCISSIST

There are many "toxic people" in the world. Individuals who for no rent or reason believe that they're superior over others and cause pain to others through cruel comments, actions, and other aggressive behavior. Narcissists, along with sociopaths and psychopaths, are one of these "toxic people." People with narcissism have an inflated sense of their own self, a depthless need for attention and admiration, a lack of empathy for anyone around them, and troubled relationships. Behind all this vain pride lies a fragile ego, and when this ego is bruised—even by the slightest critical comment—narcissists lash out with extreme prejudice against their aggressor. These individuals usually have problems in many parts of their lives, for example, in their work, family, romantic relationships, and financial affairs.

If not given the admiration of people—any people—these people become morose and angry and display their anger by being cruel and sadistic towards others, causing significant damage to those close to them. A narcissist can be your dad, mom, sister, brother, aunt, uncle, cousin, grandparent, boyfriend, girlfriend, friend, husband, wife, colleague, boss, teacher, or anyone else who is in close contact with you.

There is a common stereotype that only men are narcissists; however, that is entirely incorrect. There are quite a few women who cause immense emotional harm to their significant others. But, the main difference between a female narcissist and a male narcissist is that the woman is calculating and sneaky, whereas a male narcissist isn't. Though, this isn't to say that male narcissists aren't capable of being shrewd or cunning but merely that they are *usually* not very covert at all. On the other hand, women are known as the dangerous of the two sexes, which makes them so sharp at causing damage to their partners, friends, families, or anyone who causes them injury. However, this can also be taken with a grain of salt as women can also be very aggressive towards those they abuse too.

Yet, no matter hail or high wind, male abusers hold prominence in our culture. Domestic violence creates more victims than any other abusive psychological disorder. Survivors are literally terrorized in their own homes by their abusers. If they try to protect themselves and their children from their abusers, they are often seen as hysterical, unstable, or crazy. Without knowing the appropriate terms to describe what happened to them, survivors sound obsessed and unstable. This is why it is so important to learn how to explain the harm that occurred to them or someone else near them in incorrect terms. Gaining knowledge is the first step on the path of self-healing.

Like all other abusive personalities, narcissists have a broad spectrum of behaviors, which take many shapes and personalities. This means that some people may display few, even healthy, narcissistic traits, while others may have a full-blown clinical personality disorder. Levels of narcissism can also vary over time, situations, and life events. However, it is essential to remember that the core pattern of thinking found in the behavior of all narcissistic abusers is their need for excessive admiration and a sense of entitlement.

Almost all people exhibit narcissistic tendencies during their lives. We are all narcissists to a degree. If we enjoy our work, or lives, our families, we feel a degree of self-involvement that is desirable and healthy. Healthy narcissism is adaptive and empathic. Every human being needs admiration and attention; everyone desires success and love, and we all occasionally experience a lack of empathy. Often, we display narcissistic qualities that hurt other people's feelings or push their boundaries, usually classifying these experiences as the result of someone being aggressive, egotistical, selfish, or insensitive. These are *temporary* experiences. The person *has* the capacity to change their behavior.

The problem truly begins when significant impairments in the functionality of an individual's personality become evident. In other words, narcissism becomes a concern when the degree of self-absorption of the individual stands in the way of their awareness of the personal needs, intentions, and subjective feelings of others. They become excessively attention-seeking (as in, they want all the attention on them), view themselves as exceptional without any accomplishment, ignore the needs and wants of other people (often stepping on them to get their way), are rigid (are stable) and maladaptive, and display interpersonal entitlement, explosiveness, envy, and arrogance. These are the classic symptoms of NPD—the name given to the disorder that occurs when narcissistic tendencies become malignant.

Erich Fromm posited that narcissism becomes malignant for the individual when an individual's willfulness becomes extreme when their self-involvement reaches a level that they seem totally uncritical of themselves and are incapable of responding maturely towards criticism.

When people have NPD, they care not for anybody but themselves. They are obnoxious and have little to no empathy for the plight of others. They feel entitled to get the best of everything, all the while looking down on those who show admiration for them. These qualities impair their daily function, yet very few seek treatment for the disorder either because they don't care to get it or notice its effects on both others and themselves.

WHY IS IT CALLED NARCISSISM?

The mental disorder narcissism is named after the handsome young Greek figure who fell in love with his own reflection and was conceited, entitled, arrogant—a youth who believed in his superiority over others until his end. He was proud and disdained those who loved him, causing them irreparable harm. He was fixated and elated with himself and his physical appearance.

This disorder is named after this mythical Greek figure because this young man cared only for himself, exhibiting the quality all people of his ilk did then and do now. The lesson in this myth is that narcissism is a part of human society (because many people are like Narcissus in the world) and that it causes devastating harm to those who exhibit it. And due to radical individualism—when everybody places his/her interests, wants, and needs before others, there are even more such people in existence at this time.

WHO WAS NARCISSUS?

Narcissus, a mythical Greek demi-god renowned for his beauty, was the son of the god Cephissus and the nymph Liriope. It was said that Narcissus would live to old age if he never looked at himself. Yet, as he grew up, he gained many admirers charmed by his beauty. However, secure in his beauty and general superiority over others, he rejected them all. Many of them took their own lives because they couldn't live with the disdain and contempt Narcissus showed them. As told by Ovid in his work *Metamorphoses*, one of his admirers, Echo, a mountain nymph, encounters Narcissus and falls in love with him. He rejects her advances and leaves her heartbroken. Echo, upset by his rejection, leaves the world under herself and becomes an echo.

When Nemesis, the goddess of retribution and revenge, learned what had happened, she was enraged and decided to punish Narcissus for his conceited behavior. She took him to a pool of water, in which he caught an image of himself and, not realizing it is his reflection, fell in love with it. So, from then on, he would peer into various lakes and reflective surfaces, chancing for a look at the beautiful stranger. The more he gazed into the eyes of his reflection, the deeper he fell in love. Eventually, he finally realized that the person he saw was his own reflection, someone who would never be able to reciprocate his love. Thus, in despair at the hand fate had dealt him, he looked at himself until his death.

NARCISSISM STATISTICS

Mainly, the prevalence of narcissistic personality disorder remains largely poorly defined due to a lack of research literature. But, a few studies do provide some common statistics. According to a systematic review of various studies on the prevalence of narcissistic personality disorder done by Nikhil Dhawan, Mark E. Kunik et al. in 2009, the mean prevalence of

NPD was 1.06% with a range of 0% to 6.2%. The review concluded a very low prevalence of NPD in adult nonclinical samples. The exceptionally low mean value hints at the rarity of an NPD diagnosis.

Another study by Sigmund Karterud, Maria Øien, and Geir Pederson in 2010 supported the conclusion that NPD is a rare personality disorder. Data collected from 2277 patients—80% of whom had a personality disorder—admitted in The Norwegian Network of Psychotherapeutic Day Hospitals showed that only 0.8% of those patients had NPD. Surprisingly, the study also found that male patients were overrepresented on both the criteria and the diagnostic level.

This overrepresentation of men in NPD diagnosis was also noticed by Frederick S. Stinson, Deborah A. Dawson, Rise B. Goldstein et al. in the study they published on the prevalence of DSM-IV narcissistic personality disorder. The study, done by conducting face-to-face interviews with 34 653 adults who participated in the Wave 2 National Epidemiologic Survey on Alcohol and Related Conditions, found that the prevalence of lifetime NPD for both sexes was 6.2%, with higher rates for men at 7.7% and women at 4.8% respectively. They also found that NPD was more prevalent among younger adults, Black men and women, Hispanic women, and single/separated/divorced/widowed and never-married adults. They also found that men who had NPD had a higher chance of mental disability than women.

Later studies gave weight to this representation as they confirmed that NPD is more commonly found in males than in females because of all those diagnosed with the disorder, almost 50%—75% were male.

The American Psychiatric Publishing Textbook of Personality Disorders estimates that NPD is present in 0.5% of the United States population and in 2-16% of those people who seek help from a mental health professional.

In *Narcissistic Personality Disorder: Facing DSM-V,* Ronningstam states that more than 6% of the forensic population and 20% of the military population of the United States exhibits actual NPD and narcissistic traits as well.

WHAT IS NARCISSISTIC PERSONALITY DISORDER OR NARCISSISM?

According to the American Psychiatric Association's *Diagnostic and Statistical Manual of Mental Disorders,* Fifth Edition, DSM-5, Narcissistic Personality Disorder is defined as a stable and long-term "pervasive pattern of grandiosity (in fantasy or behavior), need for admiration, and lack of empathy, beginning by early adulthood and present in a variety of contexts." (American Psychiatric Association, 2013.) In other words, people with NDP are self-absorbed and place their self needs and wants before others. People who are clinically diagnosed with NDP display significant stable personality impairments and problems with interpersonal relationships.

NDP is also one of the least studied personality disorders; thus, there is a large amount of confusion regarding the viability, specificity, and validity of the diagnostic criteria and the prevalence of the disorder. Due to this lack of research literature, NDP was nearly omitted from the DSM-5, but after massive backlash from the clinical and research community, the decision was reversed.

As written in the DSM-5, the pattern of NDP is indicated by the presence of five (or more) of the following nine factors in an individual.

1. A grandiose sense of self-importance, i.e., exaggerating achievements and talents, wishes to be recognized as superior without any extraordinary achievements.
2. A preoccupation with fantasies of limitless success, brilliance, power, ideal love, or beauty.
3. The belief that the individual is "special" and unique and can only be understood by, seen to associate with, other special or high-status people (or groups).
4. An excessive need for admiration.
5. A sense of entitlement, i.e., unreasonable expectations of favorable treatment from others or want for automatic compliance shown by others towards the individual's expectations.

6. Constant interpersonal exploitation, i.e., takes advantage of other people to achieve their own needs.
7. Complete lack of empathy: doesn't or is not willing to recognize or sympathize with the feelings and needs exhibited by others.
8. The belief that others are envious of the individual or being jealous of others themselves.
9. Arrogant, haughty, stuck-up behavior or attitude.

These criteria are unchanged from the previous *DSM* edition. However, it should be noted a new model of NPD has been proposed in which a person with NPD is characterized based on two things: one, impairment in personality function, and two, pathologic personality traits.

In this new model, NPD is characterized by moderate or more significant impairment in personality (self and interpersonal) function, exhibited by characteristic difficulties in two or more of the following four areas.

- **Identity**—Excessive reliance on others for self-definition and maintaining self-esteem; exaggerated sense of self-importance, or oscillating between behavioral extremes—from depression to mania; emotional stability that is dependent on self-esteem.
- **Self-direction**—Setting goals based on gaining approval from others; personal standards that are incredibly high (unreasonable due to overestimation of

abilities) or extremely low (due to sense of entitlement).
- **Empathy**—Over- or underestimating the effect they have on other people; impaired ability to identify with or recognize the needs and feelings of other people; being excessively attuned to people's reactions if they're considered relevant to the self.
- **Intimacy**—Superficial relationships, especially those pursued for self-esteem regulation; little to no genuine interest in someone else's experiences; a predominant need for personal gain in every relationship pursued by the individual.

NPD is characterized by the presence of both of the following pathological personality traits:

- **Grandiosity:** Self-centeredness; belief that the individual is better than anyone else; condescending behavior; feeling entitled.
- **Attention-seeking:** Seeking admiration; excessive attempts to become the center of attention.

Broad Categories of Behavior

The aforementioned diagnostic criteria may cause a narcissistic person to display many qualities unique to their disorder, such as:

- Due to their grandiose sense of self-importance, narcissistic people constantly overestimate their abilities and inflate their accomplishments. In contrast, they often devalue the achievements of others to make themselves seem better in comparison. They are often boastful and pretentious, thinking of others beneath them.
- They are often obsessed with fantasies about power, intelligence, success, and beauty and lament the "long overdue" admiration that should've been theirs.
- They believe that they're superior, special, or unique and that others should recognize their superiority or uniqueness. Due to this arrogance, narcissistic people feel that only a few people understand them; therefore, they should only associate with them.
- Individuals with this disorder believe that their needs and wants trump the needs and wants of others—they are entitled and selfish.
- These people enhance their self-esteem by giving idealized value to everything they have—they perceive everything as more than it is, which is why their self-esteem is very fragile.
- They may be preoccupied with their impression and image and may need constant uplifting comments in order to maintain their sense of self.
- They have unreasonable expectations of kindly or accommodating behavior from other people and

become furious or frustrated when this doesn't happen. For example, these people may not feel that they have to stand in line because they're very important, so they'll try to walk to the front of the line. When people don't respond to their foolery with pride and admiration, narcissistic people get angry.

- Narcissistic people are insensitive towards others, which may cause them to exploit their fellow human beings—consciously or unconsciously. They may demand whatever they feel they should be given, no matter the cost to others.
- They form friendships, acquaintances, or romantic relationships only if the other person advances their purposes or self-esteem.
- They may assume that people close to them are worried about their welfare, prompting them to discuss their concerns with others at length, all without recognizing the feelings and needs of others—needs and feelings that they're often contemptuous of.
- They are often emotionally cold to others and show a lack of interest in anything but themselves.
- They are often envious of other people or think that other people are envious of them.
- When confronted by the possessions or successes of others, they may feel that they deserve those achievements or admiration, and when they don't get

them, they often harshly devalue the individual for his accomplishments.
- They insist on having the best of everything because they believe they're special.
- They are arrogant, snobbish, disdainful, and often condescending.
- Their fragile self-esteem makes it hard for them to take criticism. They may be haunted by their disappointing attitude or failure and may feel degraded, humiliated, or hollow, prompting them to act awfully towards others.
- Narcissistic people often have a problem maintaining interpersonal relationships because of their entitlement, need for admiration, and disregard for others.

At the same time, people with narcissistic personality disorder have trouble handling criticism or anything they think of as criticism, to which they can:

- Feel easily slighted and start to have a problem in relationships with the critic
- Get angry or act contemptuously towards the other person in order to make them appear beneath them
- Have secret feelings of shame, humiliation, vulnerability, hollowness, and vulnerability

- Feel depressed and moody because they couldn't reach perfection
- Struggle with their emotions and behavior
- Experience major problems with dealing with managing stress
- Become impatient as to why they didn't receive special treatment

HOW TO DIFFERENTIATE NARCISSISM FROM OTHER PERSONALITY DISORDERS

Several personality disorders have quite a few features in common, which makes it very important to distinguish between these disorders in order to issue a correct diagnosis. However, if an individual meets the criteria for more than one personality disorder, they may have that disorder along with NPD.

The most helpful feature that can be used to separate NPD from borderline histrionic or antisocial personality disorder is the grandiosity characteristic displayed by individuals with NPD. The lack of self-destructiveness and impulsivity and the stability of self-image displayed by a narcissistic individual also distinguish NPD from other personality disorders.

Even though all individuals with histrionic, borderline, and narcissistic personality disorder need attention, individuals with NPD require attention to be adoring and admiring. Excessive pride in accomplishments, emotional coldness, and disdain for the needs of others can also distinguish NPD from other personality disorders.

Narcissistic people lack the "history of conduct disorder in childhood or criminal behavior in adulthood" that is part and parcel of antisocial personality disorder. In both NDP and obsessive-compulsive personality disorder, the afflicted individual may be a perfectionist and believe that nobody can do better than themselves. Yet, people with OCPD are self-critical and know that they can't achieve perfection, whereas those with NPD believe that they have achieved perfection.

Many successful people display narcissistic personality traits, but these traits should only be considered as indications of NPD if they are persistent, cause significant functional impairment, and are inflexible.

CAN A NARCISSIST CHANGE?

One prevalent misconception about narcissistic people is that they are incapable of empathy and thus incapable of change. This is simply not true. Anybody can change if they put the will into it. But it is far more challenging for a narcissist to change, even if they put their will, as much as they can, to it. Narcissists are capable of empathy, but only if they put in the arduous effort of knowing themselves at the deepest level, facing the problems with their behavior and the loneliness and insecurity that hides beneath their grandiose exterior, and it is this empathy that can help them change.

Sometimes some people with NDP don't change because they don't put in enough effort or don't desire to change at their core. Narcissists, at their center, are single-minded and often believe that they're never wrong. Getting over this sentiment is very, very hard. If a narcissist can realize that they're wrong, only then can they actually take the first step towards making a change in themselves.

Starting therapy and counseling is half the battle. Narcissists can learn how to manage themselves, identify behavioral problems within themselves, set behavioral goals, gain insights into themselves, improve the quality of their relationships, improve their self-esteem, and steel themselves against harsh criticism by going to therapy. Therapy can be debilitating because it can make a person with NDP feel powerless or constantly poked with needles. Still, once the rapport is established between the therapist and the patient, the process becomes more manageable.

The willingness to change is vital if one *wants* to change within themselves. A sponge doesn't soften until it's soaked. Similarly, a narcissist needs to be soaked in therapy to change. If they don't have the capacity to do so, they will never change.

Is There a Test for Narcissism?

While there are dozens, if not hundreds, of narcissism quizzes online, none of them are supported by clinical research and are, thus, mostly inaccurate. Some can misdiagnose a person with diseases they do not have. Others can mislabel what narcissism is entirely. Therefore, an individual should always seek a therapist's opinion if they think or feel that they have a personality disorder.

There are some clinically approved personality tests that an individual can attempt to see if they have any personality disorder. However, there is no specific clinically approved narcissistic personality disorder test.

The tests include:

- Personality diagnostic questionnaire-4 (PDQ-4).
- Millon clinical multiaxial inventory III (MCMI-III).
- International personality disorder examination (IPDE).

Most people diagnosed with NDP aren't assigned the diagnosis through a test; instead, they're assigned it through extensive counseling and therapy sessions with psychiatrists, counselors, and psychologists.

IS THERE A TREATMENT?

A narcissistic personality disorder is a challenging syndrome because it is hard to treat, has a variable presentation, and complicates the treatment of disorders that occur with it. No standardized psychological or pharmacological treatment has been established for people with narcissistic personality disorder due to a lack of research into NPD. Clinical practices for NPD have yet to be formulated because the defensiveness and lack of acknowledgment of problems and vulnerabilities shown by individuals with NPD make psychotherapeutic engagement with them very difficult. Furthermore, in patients with other major personality disorders co-occurring besides NPD, the likelihood of treatment dropout increases.

Current recommendations are based mainly on clinical experience and theoretical formulations regarding treatments that specifically target NPD. Case reports suggest that these treatments can be effective for some individuals with NPD. They also offer that consistent, long-term patient care—usually involving psychotherapy and medication management—is the best approach for the treatment of NPD. The most influential of these reports focus on developing a relationship between the therapist and the individual with NDP. This means that long-term counseling is the primary treatment for NPD.

Psychotherapy

People with NPD are notoriously difficult to engage in treatment. This increases the importance of building a therapeutic alliance with mutually agreed goals between the clinician and the patient. This is why individual psychotherapy is usually the recommended method for treatment of NPD, but the nuance of the term changes depending on which school of thought you choose. Otto Kernberg states that a therapist has to eradicate or diminish the patient's NPD through confrontation in one school of thought. In contrast, in the other, Heinz Kohut suggests that the therapist's job is to encourage the patient's grandiosity in order to supplement their self-esteem.

Therapists, nowadays, use a combination of both stances to help patients recover from NPD. Therapists recognize the self-preserving role of narcissism in a patient's life and strive to help them gain a realistic understanding of their behavior. This therapy works mainly because it focuses on both the emotions and beliefs that drive NDP and narcissistic tendencies exhibited by a person. The rapport developed between a therapist and a patient can bring insight to the patient to help them change their behavior in the long term.

Other Kinds of Therapy

Usually, individual psychotherapy is recommended for the treatment of NDP. Still, other therapeutic procedures such as group, family, couples therapy, and cognitive-behavioral therapy (CBT) can also be used to treat narcissistic personality disorder. Group therapy was initially assumed to be unsuitable because it required empathy and the ability to relate to others—qualities lacking in individuals with NDP. Yet, further research suggests that group therapy can actually benefit individuals with NDP because it can help them explore their boundaries, develop trust, increase self-awareness, and receive and accept feedback—which most people with NDP lack.

A systematic review of the narcissistic personality disorder done by Eve Caligor, Kenneth N. Levy, and Frank E. Yeomans in 2015, suggested that mentalization-based therapy—when patients are taught to cultivate self-awareness, transference-focused psychotherapy—identifies patient's treatment goals and establishes an improvement contract between therapist and patient, and schema-focused psychotherapy—a work-intensive form of treatment which encourages patients to confront their narcissistic cognitive distortions and focuses on activating emotional senses—can be used to target underlying psychological issues and features of narcissistic personality disorder. The review also suggests that dialectical behavioral therapy—a treatment usually used for borderline personality disorder and self-destructive behaviors—and all other borderline personality disorder treatments with adaptations for narcissistic personality disorder can help a person with NDP.

Medications

Medications can also be used to treat narcissistic personality disorder, especially in patients who show severe narcissistic characteristics or are a danger to themselves and others. These patients can benefit from medication that reduces anxiety, impulse control issues, depression, and mood control. Medications that benefit an individual with narcissistic personality disorder are:

- Antidepressants such as sertraline and paroxetine;
- Antipsychotics such as risperidone and aripiprazole; and
- Mood stabilizers such as lithium.

NARCISSISTS IN LOVE AND RELATIONSHIPS

As mentioned before, narcissism lies on a continuum. Some narcissistic people are very obnoxious, arrogant, snobbish, and think the world of themselves. In contrast, others are shy, have no want for the achievements of others, and only want to feel good about themselves. In other words, there are extremes to narcissism, and people exist on both ends of those extremes.

When narcissism is severe, the individual may be incredibly selfish and unable to profess and express love to those they are in a relationship with. Milder forms of narcissism allow expressions of love. However, most of the time, that is not so.

Narcissists are rigid, self-serving, arrogant, and entitled. They are egocentric perfectionists—they cannot accept any error made by them. People with NPD have difficulty listening to other people's complaints against them. Since they believe that they're so special, it becomes hard for them to rationalize that they've made a mistake. This headstrong attitude is further compounded by a narcissist's inability to understand the feelings, wants, and needs of others. They constantly step on proverbial toes and blindside people—sometimes unwittingly and at other times wittingly. They believe that their needs and wants trump the needs and wants of others and that they are entitled to the best of everything due to their impressive ability to do nothing.

When a high-spectrum narcissist enters into a relationship, most of the time, it is superficial because they're unable to acknowledge the needs of their significant other over themselves—they are not able to look past their arrogance and self-absorption to give back to their partner. They honestly and sincerely believe that their wants and needs are more important than the needs of those they profess to love, and in their haste to get what they want, high-spectrum narcissists do not hesitate to step over their loved ones.

When we fall for someone, we show active concern for our significant other's life no matter where they are. We try to understand our partner's perspective, understand them, what makes them what they are, and how they differ. We offer them respect, attention, understanding, acceptance, and kindness. We offer them our time, and we love them for who they are rather than what they could be. We listen to their words, and we hold them as our equals. We empathize with them when they're weak and hold their hand when they're strong.

On the other hand, narcissists have no desire to do any of this. They seek self-gratification and work only for their gain—more success, adoration, admiration, more renown, etc. They aren't motivated to know and understand those they're in a relationship with. Instead, they often look at the adoring eyes of their partner and preen with the knowledge that they're adored and desired. This admiration bolsters their low self-esteem, and for a time, the narcissist lover is accommodating and careful. They want that admiration and adoration, and they would do anything to get it—lie, cheat, harm, anything. But when the going goes hard, they realize the effort they would have to put into gaining the same adoration, so they either leave their partner or get their fix elsewhere.

People with narcissistic personality disorder lack empathy; meaning that they're "unwilling to recognize or identify with the feelings and needs of others." (APA, 2013) This means that they have significantly impaired *emotional empathy*—the ability to express care and concern for someone's emotional state. They do, however, possess *cognitive empathy*—the ability to take someone else's perspective. The catch here is that narcissists will not use this skill until they believe it serves their needs.

Narcissists do not see others or themselves clearly. They think of other people as extensions of themselves, rather than separate individuals with separate lives, loves, needs, and desires. They are so consumed by themselves that they become oblivious to others. They also overestimate their emotional empathy and run themselves into tricky situations to get out of. To regulate their emotions and self-esteem, they distort their perception of others and their interactions with them.

They project the unwanted and harmful aspects of themselves onto others and use entitlement, self-promotion, and narcissistic abuse such as blame, contempt, criticism, and aggressions to ward off shame and vulnerability. Perfectionistic narcissists are very hard to please because they put others down on their whim, try to destroy their enemies or those who criticize them in order to maintain the illusion of perfection, and abuse those closest to them to get what they want.

These actions impair the narcissists' capacity to see the reality of things from the other person's point of view, including the love they hold for the narcissist. Therefore, in essence, a narcissist's cognitive intelligence/empathy helps them exploit others to their own ends. In contrast, their impaired emotional empathy stops them from feeling the pain they inflict on others.

This means that in order to feel better and more joyous, narcissists manipulate and exploit others. They love themselves through others by abusing them.

Narcissist Partner

Real love is a union of two individuals—a complete, equal partnership. Not romance and not codependency. Love requires us to see another person as something separate but equal to ourselves. We wish to know, encourage, love, support, understand, and see happiness. When someone loves someone, they think of their needs before their own, take pleasure in their joy, and try not to hurt them. The love of a partner should be like this: absolute, resplendent with happiness, and selfless.

With a narcissistic partner, love is not taken as love anymore; and instead, it is taken as possession. The significant other becomes an extension of the narcissistic partner, who ruthlessly exploits them for his own gain. People who are usually starved for expressions of love, such as words of affirmation, gifts, acts of service, physical touch, and emotional and moral support, love narcissistic people because they at least get some kind of love from them. Even though narcissistic people are remote, dismissive, or aggressive, they give their partners the love they want for a short time. But, it is best to remember that NPD exists on a continuum from mild to malignant with cruel behavior, and the more severe it is, the greater the demands of the relationship.

A narcissistic partner with a clinically diagnosed NDP is emotionally unstable. Sometimes he may show love when he is motivated or when his needs are met. At other times, he may be violent, sadistic, cruel, and demeaning because his needs haven't been fulfilled, or he sees no point in being nice to you anymore. Such a partner may always compare the relationship you both have with the relationship your friends have. If your friend made up with her boyfriend even when he was cruel to his partner, then your partner will also ask you to do the same. Some narcissists may even complain that you're unlike the partner of another friend they have. They may compare your qualities with theirs just to make you feel horrible about yourself. This is a blatant show of a narcissist's lack of empathy. They don't feel the turmoil they're causing you; they only think about themselves and no one else, not even you.

Sometimes your partner may say horrible things about you to keep you in your place. They may focus on your failures rather than your wins to keep you dependent on them, make you ask them for their advice, and make themselves look superior. They feel like their wants and needs should be above your wants and needs. If they want something, you should get it for them. If they want you now, then you should be there for them. At other times, they may demean you because they need to remove some of their negative emotions, and you're just a convenient solution. A tissue that, after use, could be discarded easily.

Narcissistic partners love to be painted in a pleasing light. Their main objective is to be admired and adored. They want adoration, and they will do anything to get it. If you say something they hadn't thought of before, they may even snap at you, telling you that what you're saying is a terrible idea, only to repeat it to someone as their original idea, to gain the respect and admiration they want. They may exaggerate their accomplishments for that heady rush of pleasure when people look at them with respect. They may snap at you in private and praise you in public because they wish to be seen as a man who loves his partner, all to gain attention and admiration.

In relationships, both partners are supposed to uplift and support each other. But in a relationship with a narcissist, this doesn't happen. A narcissist may try to make you jealous of their skills, of the people who admire them, of their entitlement, of their accomplishments, and success because they're intimidated by your skills, success, beauty, charisma, and intelligence. They may become so jealous and envious that they'd destroy your possessions behind your back, all because they feel that what you had accomplished should've been theirs by right. This jealousy can reach its limit when they try to destroy your reputation, so you may not gain more of everything they want. They may even become jealous of their child when you give them the attention your narcissistic partner wants for himself.

A narcissistic person has, first and foremost, a low level of self-esteem, so any slight, no matter how small, feels like a hurricane to them. If you don't pay them attention, they may do drastic things to regain it. If you don't fit their idea of the perfect partner, you may be criticized at every point. If you meet with some male friends or female friends, you may be the object of scrutiny and uncomfortable questions and insinuations of cheating. They may even go as far as to turn your support system against you by telling lies about the problems you make in your relationship with him. When you ask why they're being paranoid and explain that you'll never be unfaithful, they may blame everything on you. They may make unfair comparisons between him and your friends and constantly think that you'll be unfaithful to them one day.

A person with NPD expects special treatment because they think they're exceptional. They elevate themselves above others and distance themselves from those they deem "unworthy" or not "unique enough" for them. They may want everything done according to their specifications without caring for the effects of their actions and demands on others.

In the end, people with NPD demoralize, criticize, exploit, manipulate, blame, erode your trust, and demean you at every turn. They may speak over you, believing that they have superior ideas. They may interrupt when you're speaking or making a point in order to say something wholly pointless. They may reject you countless times, only to make those rejections your fault, and they may also, at their extreme, cut you off from the world until you're at their mercy, unstable and insecure and dependent on them for everything.

They Often End Up Lonely

Due to their unflinching self-absorption, entitlement, arrogance, egotism, pretentiousness, and lack of empathy, many narcissists are eventually left alone. Their partners, after getting fed up with their constant need for attention, admiration, and their antics, leave them to pursue a better life. Some narcissists who learn to manage their emotions and instabilities live a better life with kids, spouses, and friends. However, others who were ridiculously awful to everyone throughout their younger years may end up lonely most of all.

According to a study conducted by Gregory L. Carter and Melanie D. Douglas on aging narcissism conducted in 2018 on a total of 100 middle-aged and 100 older-aged participants—who competed on the 40-item Narcissistic Personality Inventory and the UCLA Loneliness Scale, Version 3, found that older-age participants (around 70 years old) had lower levels of narcissism and higher levels of loneliness than middle-aged (around 48 years old) participants. The study concluded that narcissism moderates loneliness and that the higher the narcissism, the lower the loneliness.

THE NARCISSIST AND THEIR FAMILY

A narcissist family is one where the needs and wants of the parent/s are the family's primary focus. Everybody, the children and the other spouse, have to meet the demands of the narcissistic partner/s. In worse cases, the children support and fulfill the orders made by the parent. For example, if the parent asks the clean and shiny floor to be cleaned again, the child has to do it. Otherwise, he'll face punishment. If the parent tells a young child to start washing clothes because the parent's hands will get ruined, then the child has to do that or else. If the parent asks the child to do an impossible task and the child fails, the parent will take out his anger on the child by either emotionally or physically abusing them.

Like all other abnormal and dysfunctional families, there is abuse and denial of said abuse in a narcissistic family. The children and or the spouse are neglected, their boundaries disrespected, bear cold and arrogant behavior, live in secrecy, live through explosive conflicts and punishments, and deprived of emotional validation. In such a family, unspoken rules are applied to everybody, which can be: take sides, someone has to be blamed, be submissive to your parents, feelings are wrong, image is more important than self and much more.

There are some stereotypical roles in the family of a narcissist parent, such as:

Enabler: The spouse or a daughter who tends to the basic needs of the narcissist and keeps a solid front. The enabler also makes excuses for the narcissist's actions because they want approval and acceptance from the narcissist.

Flying monkey: A flying monkey can be a friend, a family member, child, spouse, or even a work colleague. These people are the ones who make sure the commands of the narcissistic parent are enforced—they are an enforcer of the edicts issued by the parent. They use various abusive techniques to fulfill their purpose. They make the other person feel weak and horrible, and they often think that the narcissistic person is doing everything right.

Scapegoat: The scapegoat can be a child (oldest or most outspoken child) on whom the narcissistic parent vents out his anger. The child can be physically, emotionally, and psychologically abused by his parents due to slights not even committed by him. A scapegoat may also be abused by his siblings, who follow the narcissist's lead to stay safe from the beating or abuse.

Golden child: This child is one the narcissist thinks matches his own image. The child can be the oldest or second-oldest; however, selection depends entirely on intelligence, ability, beauty, talent, and the narcissist's agenda. If the narcissist values beauty, they'll select the most beautiful child. If they want talent and intelligence, then they'll choose the most intelligent of their offspring. The narcissist favors the golden child, gives him everything, and feeds him the lie that he is better than his own siblings. The narcissist grooms the child to take his place one day.

In such an abusive household, everything revolves around the narcissistic parent. If the parent is the sun, then its children are in orbit around it, always there for admiration and a testament to the sun's strength. For the parent, their family is a status symbol and a tool that they can use to do anything for themself. If anyone of their family members breaks the image of the family, they are punished, physically and verbally attacked, and ridiculed. Children can be discarded as easily as a used napkin by the parent and taken up as quickly again.

When the parent assigns roles to each family member, he inadvertently makes the family members compete against each other to stay safe. Every child is left fighting for the toe-hold they could claim. This practice delivers great harm to the children's psyche, resulting in issues that rear their heads later in life. These children have no idea what love is, what acceptance, sharing, and respect are, and what a happy family actually is. After years of fighting tooth-and-nail for everything, they have no idea how to live in the real world. They had no idea how to feel the emotion and had no idea how to deal with their constant anxiety and ensuring depression.

These children don't trust anyone due to their cut-throat upbringing, have no idea what intimacy or love are, and do not know how to live in a world separate from their abusive parents.

In the end, a narcissistic parent does so much harm to their family that it takes decades of therapy to lighten it. Sometimes, the children who have been through the horror cannot bear to live with themselves and kill themselves. At other times, they go into such a deep depression that it's hard to get them out of it. At still other times, many children have no idea how to deal with the unknown world, so they go back to the one they know, making the process of narcissistic abuse continue until it is stopped or until they change themselves.

THE NARCISSISTS' EFFECTS ON THEIR CHILDREN

At the best of times, handling a narcissistic person is challenging to handle. That is by an adult, so for a child undergoing the ministrations of a narcissistic parent can be highly unpredictable and upsetting. Narcissistic people lack emotional empathy, but they have cognitive empathy in spades. This means that while they cannot lend emotional support to someone, it is easy for them to understand someone's point of view; they can manipulate, exploit, and understand and care for other people by using this cognitive empathy.

Narcissistic parenting can have adverse and traumatic long-term effects on children that can impact their whole lives. Just like adult narcissists leave marks on those they end up in relationships with, they also leave marks on their own children. Due to the lack of emotional empathy and understanding, narcissists do more significant harm to their own children than their spouses. A child with a narcissistic parent will not be seen or heard—their wants and needs will not be fulfilled because the narcissistic parent doesn't consider the child a separate human being with its own needs and wants. The child's point of view, arguments, and feelings will not be acknowledged or taken into consideration by the parent (again, due to the parent's arrogance and self-centeredness), and they will be valued more for the amount of work they can do rather than who they are to the parent.

The child will be taught that his image is more important than reality, that he should keep secrets to protect the family and the parent, that he shouldn't trust others because they will always betray him. Children who have gone through years of narcissistic parenting trust no one as they have been manipulated and exploited so often that they're wary of everyone. They have been there for the parent—holding their hair when they vomited and cleaned up after them, criticized and judged so much that they have no sense of self anymore, forced to grow very fast, and emotionally undeveloped.

Such a child may not be taught the appropriate boundaries necessary for survival. They may grow up frustrated because of the lack of love and attention they never got from their parent and may believe that they are not worthy of love from anyone.

Some children may even suffer from post-traumatic stress disorder, depression, and even debilitating anxiety when they grow up. They may require trauma recovery due to the constant shaming and humiliation done to them by their parent. They may not even know right from wrong and may have lost their sense of self and ability to make independent decisions at the hands of their narcissistic parent, who abused them for years.

Being raised by a narcissistic parent causes psychological and emotional damage to the child's psyche that is long-lasting, even well into adulthood. Even if their parent seems charming to other people, they aren't good for the child. When the child makes a mistake, as all children inevitably do, then their parent might be abusive towards them, blaming the child for bringing the punishment upon themselves. As a result, the child might grow up believing that they are responsible for the wrong actions of their parent because they're too naughty, too headstrong, or too slow in their work. They never learn that their parent is the problem, not them. And when they do, it is usually too late because the emotional and psychological scars are there to stay.

2

DEALING WITH A NARCISSIST

A narcissistic abuser feels that he is powerful—that he has control over his victim. Yet, his ugliness and contempt for those he cannot break give him this power. His hatred for others fuels his contempt, driving him to deeper ends of the lake of evil. Ultimately, hatred is meaningless and hollow and gives an individual nothing but sorrow. Therefore, any power fueled by hatred is empty as it never lasts in the long term. The only way for a victim to counter this false strength is to become stronger yourself. Recognize the patterns of behavior exhibited by a narcissist. Learn their tells to save yourself misery in yet another abusive and narcissistic relationship. A man can only do something if he understands it. Therefore, understand your enemy—and he is your enemy because he means you nothing but harm—and learn to recognize his type so you can take action when it's necessary.

Learning the narcissistic modus operandi can help you recognize the narcissistic people in your life and teach you how to deal with them.

HOW DO NARCISSISTS CHOOSE THEIR VICTIMS?

Remember that narcissists choose their victims. You don't spontaneously fall into a relationship with a narcissist. Instead, they inspect the value you would potentially create for them, and then they invest in you.

Narcissists have a compulsive desire for admiration and adoration—they are attention-seeking and yearn for praise. Suppose a person exhibits mild narcissistic traits such as preening when praised, valuing the opinion of others to regulate their self-esteem, and wanting admiration, among others. In that case, they may be able to live an everyday functioning life. People with narcissistic personality disorder, on the other hand, don't have this luxury.

One characteristic of NPD is that it impairs an individual's personality, meaning that if someone has NPD, they cannot function properly in their community or society as a whole. They lack emotional empathy—thus, they cannot empathize or sympathize with people; they cannot see the impact of their actions on other people. This lack allows them to commit heinous crimes against their partners or those they're in contact with. But, before moving on, it is essential to remember that narcissists choose to abuse the closest and dearest people—the abuse is caused by choice; it is not a passive result of their mental illness. They consciously control all the actions they perform and are, thus, accountable for their actions.

Learning a narcissist emotional language and why and how they select their victims can help you see through the mask most of them wear around others. You can peer at their implicit cruelty, usually ingrained in their gestures, tone, facial expressions, and in the chasm of mismatch between what they say and what they do. You can become aware of their calculating and exploitive nature that is set on devaluing others, and you can learn to recognize the qualities - of each hsas many - that attract narcissistic people the most.

Narcissists tend to choose their victims through careful analysis -seeking out vulnerable points and insecurities. They are drawn to people who exhibit qualities or have accomplishments that they themselves are envious of. For example, , they'll get into a relationship with an intelligent and accomplished person in order to bolster their own image and to preen at their luck – that they could catch such a prize. The resulting admiration from people - when they see that the narcissist has such an amazing partner - will be the main focus of the narcissist.

Therefore, there is a range of qualities that a narcissist is attracted to, many of which can be both directly congruent to the narcissist personality and complementary to it at the same time. Provided below is a list of qualities that attract narcissists to their victims.

Uniqueness, Strength, Power, and Success

Narcissists are attracted to people who have qualities that they think could add value to and bolster their image. If a person looks good to others, they will inevitably make the person who walks in their shadow seem as good. Due to their attention- and validation-seeking nature, Narcissists are attracted to such people. As the saying goes, "if you can't get it, act as you have it." Narcissists take this saying to heart—they want to show themselves off as incredible, new, and glorious. Suppose they don't have the achievements to position themselves as the most brilliant, charismatic, successful, and influential people. In that case, they will attach themselves to those who have these achievements in order to get their admiration fix.

They will flatter, cajole, pay compliments, flirt, show passion, be affectionate and fond, full of goodwill and love towards the object of their attention—the person from whom they want something. They will put this person on a pedestal, fawning over everything they do to get into their lives. In turn, this person will feel valued and appreciated and, as a result, will become more open to the narcissist. Who among us doesn't love people who acknowledge our strengths and accomplishments? The answer is that anybody who is human likes to have their achievements acknowledged, which the narcissist does.

They constantly make the person they're propositioning feel amazing, and that is where things go downhill.

Narcissists will burrow into the lives of such people until they prove themselves invaluable—or until their partner becomes reliant on and blindly trusts the narcissist. The partner will believe everything the narcissist says, even if it is a lie. They will become dependent on the narcissist. If people tell them that their partner is lying or being untruthful about something, they will not believe them.

At this point in the relationship, the narcissist will have total control over their partner. Now the abuse will start. The strengths that the narcissist used to fawn over will become flaws. Before they described their partner as "intelligent," now they will tell them as a "know-it-all" or a "smartass." If they were kind before, now they will become a "bleeding-heart." The heady rush narcissists get from destroying strong, successful, and accomplished people is comparable to nothing else. After all, they think, they have successfully made these people who had everything lower than them. They delight in being the ones admired, trusted, and adored by their victim. When they break their partners, they are at the top of their game—they are malicious, manipulative, exploitative, well-versed in sadism, and exceptionally cruel.

Therefore, narcissists are attracted to strong, successful, intelligent, and accomplished people because the heady rush they get from destroying and victimizing these people is incredible—the admiration and satisfaction they get from doing this are also no less.

Naïveté, Vulnerability, and Low Self-Esteem

Directly opposite to those who are strong and independent are people who are vulnerable, naive, and have low self-esteem. The rush narcissists get from victimizing such people is as strong, if not stronger, than the rush they get from victimizing people who are independent and self-assured. This is mainly because when narcissists break people who are naïve, vulnerable, or have low self-esteem, they destroy them entirely because they become dependent on them for emotional validation. When they get none, they are left crippled and downtrodden.

When they want something from other people, narcissists can be incredibly charismatic and charming. For people who are deprived of attention, vulnerable, or think the worst of themselves, this kind of attention is powerful, addictive, and very flattering when it is aimed at them. They feel things they haven't before—they are admired by this fantastic person who sees their flaws as strengths, uplifts them at every turn, and loves them unconditionally. They fall very deeply for this charming person, unknowing that they have committed a very grave mistake.

Naïve people are usually young or have not been exposed to the world's reality very much. Such people have not been exposed to the blinding charisma that can be affected by a narcissistic person before, which is why when they fall, they fall deeply, and when they break, they shatter completely. The narcissist thrives on this shattering. They liked to be admired, loved and adored—so when someone thinks that the narcissist is their world, the narcissist is very flattered. But inevitably, as all things come to an end, so does this relationship.

Adventurousness and the Zest for Life

People who are full of life and curiosity are some of the most beautiful people in existence. They take joy in every new thing they discover. They love to find out and visit new places. They are loved by many and liked by all. They are those people who are always looking for things such as freedom, adventure, challenge, intensity, and risk, etc. Narcissists target these people because of their zest for life—these people love to live and experience things, and this zest makes them admirable, something that narcissists hunger for.

Since narcissists suffer from a pathological need for admiration, they target these people to share in the adulation they receive. They insert themselves into the lives of these people, make them dependent on themselves, and then deride, demean, and discourage them from doing what they love. Such people may find that, at first, narcissists are some of the best people they could ever spend time with—someone who meets them on their wavelength and talks to them about the issues they are passionate about. They feel this because the narcissist tries his hardest to make sure that his partner becomes reliant on him, and it is by holding this reliance hostage do narcissists sabotage and exploit those close to them.

Integrity and a Strong Sense of Morality

Since narcissists have no emotional empathy, they attach themselves to other people like emotional leeches, sucking their life out of them. People with a strong sense of integrity—who are honest—aren't usually convinced by a narcissist's two-faced charisma. They are honest with themselves and others, and when they see something that seems to them as untruthful or dishonest, they say so. These people hold themselves and others to high standards—mostly themselves.

This honesty can sometimes prove to be a poisonous pill as people who are too honest become an object of ridicule. Narcissists can capitalize on the resulting feelings of insecurity to ingratiate themselves with real people. The high-stakes battleground formed by the battle between the instincts of the honest person and what they see is something that the narcissist feels thrilled about. They engender weakness in the heart of the genuine person to make them reliant on them.

Resilience

A resilient person can bounce back from the hardest and harshest of tragedies. They have a hardy character and refuse to bow down before life events that try to crush them. Many resilient individuals have trauma in their pasts, and this trauma can sometimes leave people fragile for a time. If a narcissist person latches on to a resilient person in this time of fragility, they can cause considerable damage to their emotional and psychological well-being.

Conscientiousness and Reliability

A conscientious person follows what they think is right or true. Morals dictate their actions, which is why they put other people's welfare above their own. They are always painstakingly careful of everything, even the remarks they make or the comments they pass on other people, things, and events. They think before they speak, and they give the benefit of the doubt to those who make them angry, cross boundaries or say horrible things to them.

Narcissists capitalize on the fact that conscientious people will always believe them if they present a realistic enough picture unless proven to be a liar by someone else. They feed conscientious people lies and make them believe things that subvert morality. They are aware that such people will always do something they feel obligated to do. So, if a narcissist wants someone destroyed, they might use this unequivocal belief (that conscientious people hold) to make them do heinous things like getting someone arrested on false charges. Narcissists guilt-trip and shame conscientious people into doing something they want by pointing to the flaws in their worldview, work, or thinking patterns.

Sentimentality and Empathy

Sentimental people get emotional at the littlest of things, while empathic people sympathize with the feelings of others and may, at times, even feel what others feel. Both are more likely to forgive someone who has crossed their boundaries. Narcissists make the most out of this ability. They ingratiate themselves with sentimental and empathic people and weave sad stories about themselves, making both of these people sympathize with them. When they inevitably fall out of character, they make excuses easily accepted by these people.

Someone who is empathic is more likely to forgive someone who has hurt them irrevocably—they may even take that person back if they beg and plead enough. They may not realize, just like a sentimental person, that their partner or friend is manipulating them into doing the things they want. This objective use of the good conscience of these people (by the narcissist) can hurt their emotional and psychological well-being to the extent that they may never open to anyone ever again. This means that narcissists can damage people who are too open and too eager to meet and believe other people.

Caregiving: Those Who Offer Unconditional Love

People who offer unconditional love are selfless and think more about other people than themselves. Whether it is money, emotional support, or physical support, they offer whatever they have to people who they believe need those things. Therefore, caregiving people are some of the most open and loving people around. And it is this caring nature that wins them, admirers. Narcissistic people see the open heart of these people and the regard with which other people look at them and become jealous. All narcissists are governed by the pathological need to be admired and be the center of attention. When they don't get this attention, narcissistic people can be the cruelest people around.

When a narcissist targets a carebear—someone who loves other people and helps them without wanting anything in return—he may sabotage their relationship. They may speak lies against them to their parents and friends and make the carebear reliant on him by showing them selfless love and desire for them and whittle away their serenity by lying to them repeatedly. Narcissistic people also target caregivers because they offer unconditional love to the—love that doesn't require reciprocity. They may bathe in this love for a while without doing anything heinous. Still, sooner rather than later, they return to their original nature—which is malicious, cruel, and without empathy.

EIGHT THINGS YOU SHOULD NEVER SAY TO A NARCISSIST

1. Don't say, "It's not about you."

Narcissists want everything to be about themselves. They have a pathological need to have the admiration and adoration of other people. They think that everything that happens is because of them. If someone paid their spouse a compliment, they would preen because they believe their spouse is an extension of themselves. Therefore, it is better not to say anything like this to a narcissist because they may take it the wrong way and become defensive—or cross with you.

2. Don't say, "You're not listening."

Narcissists are self-centered people. They think of everybody close to them as an extension of themselves. They are entitled and believe that their needs triumph over the needs of others. So, when you state that they aren't listening, they definitely aren't. They are probably thinking about something more important to them—that thing is just not you. So instead of explaining what you have been through, ask them if they want to know about what your day went or how your best friend's boyfriend broke up with her, or how scientists discovered a new planet. If your partner/spouse/close narcissistic friend thinks that you're worth listening to, then he will listen. If he doesn't, well, you can't force them to listen to you.

3. Don't say, "Ina Garten did not get her lasagna recipe from you."

With arrogance comes pride, and narcissists are more prideful than most. They think that they are unique—that they are the best, most intelligent, charismatic, charming, and lovely people. They struggle with low self-esteem, which can lead them to bouts of depression, so they regulate it by spinning atrociously great stories about themselves and aggrandizing the worth of their achievements. Their pride and arrogance cocoon their fragility, so when someone takes a poke at their shield, they act out violently. Therefore, correcting a narcissist is a losing battle. Doing so would only alienate them from you and reinforce their belief that they're not good enough.

4. Don't say, "Do you think it might be your fault?"

Narcissists think that they do everything perfectly—they chase perfection and believe with all their might that they can achieve it, so much so that they bathe their fragile self-esteem with assurances that they'll do everything perfectly. Thus, when someone accuses them of doing something wrong, flawed, or imperfect, they have a meltdown because they cannot imagine that they would do something like that. This is why most narcissists, when confronted by their poor behavior, start blaming and projecting their own mistakes over the other person. Therefore, think very carefully before confronting a narcissist with the holes in their logic because the resulting explosion is just not pretty. It is destructive too.

5. Don't say, "You're being a bully."

Narcissists project their needs over others. They think they are more entitled to the best of everything, regardless of their status, class, ability, intelligence, or if they deserve that thing or not. They think the world revolves around them and that everyone should acquiesce to their demands just because. This lack of empathy also does them no favors. They cannot understand someone other than themselves; they don't understand the needs of others—neither do they want to, unless those needs benefit them in some way. They don't care for the needs of others at all—they are self-centered to the extreme. Thus, telling them point-blank that they're less than perfect is like poking a bear during hibernation—the bear is going to wake up from its slumber and eat you.

Therefore, instead of waving a red flag printed with their crimes in their face and risking them getting irritated and annoyed enough to without something from you, you should approach this problem in another way. That is, try to be more diplomatic, flatter their ego, and then tell them how their behavior is affecting their image. That will straighten them back up. Probably.

6. Don't say, "Stop playing the victim."

Narcissists will do anything to get what they want. Usually, they want admiration and all the attention they could get, but sometimes (if you're dealing with a person with high-spectrum NPD), they may wish to destroy somebody or something because they/it hurt their fragile self-esteem. At this instance, they may shop themselves as the victim in the story because it would get their point across that much quicker.

However, many times, due to their flawed personality function and lack of self-awareness, narcissists may even think that they were the victim in a situation caused by their own flawed decisions. So when people confront them with their flaws, they may hide away from them or lash out violently.

7. Don't say, "It's not a competition."

Narcissists associate with those they deem to be at their level. These people can be the best in their fields or the best overall amongst many others. Narcissists also get jealous and envious of the tiniest thing. For example, they may get jealous that their friend has a better boyfriend than them, or they may get jealous of someone's wealth or their car or their phone just because they

believe they should've had those things. This means that narcissists compete with everyone. They want to be the best, and in the race to become the best, they can step over anyone and cause as many injuries as they need to people who oppose them.

Therefore, instead of telling a narcissist to stop taking everything as a competition, learn that they cannot stop doing it. So if you want peace of mind, you're going to be the one who will have to let go of the competitive streak.

8. Don't say, "Let it go."

Narcissists take everything personally because they're perfectionists and control-freaks and cannot fathom that they will ever do something wrong. Their faith in themselves is such that it leads them into making terrible and awful decisions that backfire more than they prove to be correct. So when someone tells them to let something go, they cannot do that because their pride is pricked and because their image has been cracked. They can see that they aren't all that and that evaluation sticks in their craw because they believe themselves to be the best. Who can someone else who is not as intelligent, beautiful, or strong as they are cast judgment on them?

Therefore, rather than telling the narcissist to let the issue slide, listen to what they're talking about, soothe their tantrum and then relax after they're gone. You can't do anything to antagonize them if you want a peaceful relationship with them, so it's better to listen to an hour-long rant about someone rather than deal with a violent and mad stranger who wants to hurt the person who caused the injury.

WHAT SHOULD YOU DO IF YOU'RE IN A NARCISSISTIC RELATIONSHIP?

When they want to present themselves as kind, empathic, and understanding, narcissists can do that with aplomb; They will become the perfect partner/friend/spouse/colleague you've ever been blessed to know all your life. They will be helpful, loving, supportive, sympathetic, and kind no matter what you go through. But just like they can emulate the best qualities of humanity, they can mimic the worst of humanity too.

In a relationship, a narcissist can be both kind and savage at the same time. When you do something that they deem as good, they will be rewarding and free with their expressions of love, and when you do something that they don't like, you will be met with callous and cruel savagery straight out of your worst nightmare. For example, if you tell your partner that whatever they did was not perfect, they might become incensed and project their hates and flaws onto you. They might say hurtful, demeaning, and awful things to you in their bid to make you feel as they did. They want you to weep with fear for the awful things you said to them.

There are also other ways to deal with narcissistic people, depending on the situation and the level of anger the narcissistic person is spewing out. Some of these ways of dealing are listed below.

1. Ignore Their Ranting

Narcissists do not care for the needs of other people, so when they say hurtful things to you that you know stem from their pricked pride, you either have the choice to ignore them, respond to them, or leave them. If you still wish to pursue a relationship with the person, ignoring the words may be a solution. It is not a solution that is recommended for dealing with high-spectrum narcissistic people, but it can be used for people who display narcissistic tendencies.

2. Ascertain Your Personal Needs and Embrace Your Limitations

If you wish to remain with your spouse/partner even after you have learned that they exhibit many narcissistic tendencies, then you need to be aware of a few things, such as:

-Narcissistic people can be toxic and obnoxious when things don't go their way; if you can deal with that, you should go on with your relationship.

-Narcissistic people can also be tiring to be around. Their constant need for affection, admiration, and attention can be brain-wrecking.

-Narcissistic people always think about themselves, so if you want emotional connection or love from the relationship, you won't get it, no matter how much you want to.

-Narcissistic people are also very manipulative. They will twist your needs and emotions into a pretzel to get what they want.

If you consent to or are aware of all these potential ramifications of being in a relationship with a narcissistic person, then you may do so. However, going in, you'll have to learn some new things to manage your narcissistic partner, such as giving praise without being prompted on the slightest of achievements, offering support unequivocally, and refraining from hurting the ego of the narcissist, among others.

You will have to learn that your demands will not be met as narcissistic people will not care for yours as much as they care for themselves. Therefore, to save yourself from unnecessary heartache, you should embrace your limitations instead of bucking against them.

3. Ascertain Your Self-Worth Differently

If you're in a relationship with a narcissist, remember that they will always put themselves first. Narcissists are self-centered and care not for anybody but themselves. If you give them an inch, they will step all over you.

Therefore, if they put themselves before you, put yourself before them too. Make it clear to them that you have needs and that those needs have to be met no matter what they think. Remind them that you fulfill all their needs, so they have to acquiesce to their demands and needs too. When you make your position clear, it will become harder for the narcissist to manipulate or project their needs on you.

4. Be Compassionate and Try Your Best to Listen

Most narcissists suffer from a lack of adequate self-esteem, which is why they try their hardest to project themselves as someone larger than life to others. They chase perfection and want to appear as the embodiment of perfection to others because, in their minds, perfection is what gains them, admirers This lack of self-esteem coupled with bad judgment can land a narcissist in catastrophes, which they'll no doubt blame on someone else because they believe that other people prompted them to do what they did; they wouldn't have done anything wrong otherwise.

When narcissists are engaging in self-pity—which happens more often than not because low self-esteem leads to depression—they ruminate about all the decisions that led them to where they are now. They are expressing why the influence of such and such made them do that. They never take direct responsibility for anything as they can't believe that they would ever do something imperfectly.

Therefore, if a narcissist is expressing their doubts about themselves—which is very rare—be receptive and listen to them. They won't thank you for it; however, they may act better towards you for a bit of time after it.

5. Do Not Engage In Mind Games

Mind games are a particular skill cultivated by nearly all narcissists—after all, how could they get their daily dose of adulation if they don't manipulate people into giving it to them? They are masters at their game, so when you try to beat them at the chessboard they've been the king of for years, they'll only crush you.

Therefore, it is better not to engage your narcissistic other in mind games—learn about the mind games they use and educate yourself but don't engage in them because no matter how much you learn to push their buttons, they'll also know how to push yours. Unlike you, their reactions won't be chained by emotional empathy or any feelings for you. They will speak horrible things to you that would only hurt you in the end.

6. Understand Their Criticism for What It Is: It Is Not About You

Narcissists are some of the most selfish people wandering around the Earth. They are self-centered and care only for themselves. They project their needs over the needs of others and feel that they're entitled to the best of everything, all without any achievements or accomplishments. This projection can result in terrible fights. Since narcissists are perfectionists, they can't bear to think that they may have said or done something wrong, so in their opinion, everything that goes wrong is not their fault. It is yours. They sincerely believe that you, their childhood, abuse, their parents, their friends, or anybody—or anything—else is the cause of all their problems. Every problem they've had, such as financial difficulty, lack of friends, and irregular self-esteem, is because of other people or events.

Therefore, you have to understand that the narcissist is projecting their insecurities and their problems onto you when they are degrading, demeaning, being cruel, and savage towards you. Their problem is caused by themselves, which they're trying to pin on you—they're trying to blame you for their sins. Don't let them do it. Protect yourself from them—not by getting angry—instead, don't give them the attention they want to them due to their antics. Walk away from them when they degrade you; you are worth so much more.

7. Do Not Expect Humility from a Narcissist

Narcissists, by design, are arrogant and proud. Humility is the absence of pride. Therefore, humble a narcissist is not. A narcissistic person is boastful of their achievements, beauty, brilliance, charisma, abilities, or talent. They want to bask in the admiration of others and go to great lengths to achieve that goal. Therefore, if you see a narcissist do something good like giving charity or helping someone without being asked, know that sooner or later they will talk about what they did if only to get people to admire them for their (false or cultivated) generosity.

8. Convince the Narcissist to Believe That Your Activity Benefits Them

Narcissists have no shortage of admirers as they present different facets of themselves to everyone. To some, they're kind. To others, they may be generous, and to others still, they may be charming. Narcissists like admiration and attention, so if you give it to them, they'll bask in it as a cat does under the sun.

However, if you're affectionate and kind all the time, they'll conclude that you may be too attached to them, and if they have a malignant form of NPD, they may decide to harm you because they don't get any pleasure out of your adulation anymore. For them, the lure is gone, and to recreate that lure, they'll go to a great many lengths.

Therefore, if you want to stay in a relationship with a narcissist, you'll have to convince them of your importance. Either by being invaluable to them in some way or by doing something for them that they can't do themselves.

9. Don't Show Your Anger and Frustration; Smile as Much as Possible

People with narcissistic tendencies thrive on attention—any kind of attention. If they're projecting their insecurities on you and ranting, they want you to participate and to be angry at them. Through your participation, you show them that they are worth the trouble—that they're something more to you than just a person, and that they're deserving of your attention. It makes their ego bigger and soothes their pride.

But on the flip side, engagement also makes them livid. How dare you stand up to them? They think that their opinions, needs, and wants are superior to yours, so when you speak up against them, they feel assaulted and, predictably, lash out violently.

To avoid such volcanic eruptions, you should try to put out fires as much as possible. Don't throw fuel on the fire, rather throw water. If you love them enough to stay with them regardless of their behavior, then you'd want to live in a more peaceful atmosphere than a more crackling-with-energy-atmosphere that would burn you to cinders. Therefore, avoid exacerbating arguments and try to smile, be polite, and diplomatic as possible if you want to maintain your relationship with them.

10. Remember, You Get to Protect Yourself, and You Can Do It

Lastly, if the situation is getting out of hand, protect yourself. Nobody is going to come and save you from abuse. The narcissistic other will not relent in their assault because they cannot do so. They regard you as a flee stuck on their boot—as someone who is inconsequential. They do not care for your needs or wants and don't have the capacity to understand your emotions. All they care about is themselves and how they can achieve their own goals.

Therefore, the responsibility lies with you. If you think you need to leave before harm befalls you, do so because nobody else will be able to make that decision for you—not even your narcissistic partner. And if you decide to stay and protect yourself, you can do that too. Remember that all decisions that affect you lie in your hand. You have a choice, but it's up to you how you make it.

3

NARCISSISTIC ABUSE SYNDROME

An individual with narcissistic personality disorder (NPD) is overburdened with self-importance. They think that they're entitled to the best of everything, so they don't hesitate to crush people to get what they want. They feel superior to other people and project their needs over them. They think their wants trump the wants of anyone else and that they should get everything, even if they don't deserve it. This lack of moral adherence and self-centeredness usually translates into an arrogant, prideful, and vain behavior distinguished by its lack of empathy for anyone or anything except itself.

Narcissists can go to any length to get what they want from their victim, not even maintaining moral boundaries in their search for the object of their desire. This manipulation is both psychologically and emotionally devastating, which is why people who have been through relationships with narcissists develop symptoms of PTSD due to the trauma they go through. If a person exhibits PTSD-like symptoms, they are suffering from narcissistic abuse syndrome.

WHAT IS NARCISSISTIC ABUSE SYNDROME?

A form of Post-traumatic stress disorder, narcissistic abuse syndrome, occurs when an individual suffers from abuse perpetrated by a narcissist, specifically an individual diagnosed with NPD. The narcissistic person is emotionally abusive towards their victims, often destroying their self-esteem in the process.

People victimized by narcissists struggle with self-doubt all the time. Then they think themselves worthless, often going as far as to say that they are at fault in the relationship rather than their abusive partner. They believe that their partner treats them horribly because they are flawed, a failure, and have many shortcomings—a mentality that is encouraged by the narcissist deliberately. After all, it is far easier for the narcissist to manipulate an emotionally volatile individual than an emotionally stable person. More often than not, narcissists are the people who plant the seeds of this mentality into the minds of their victims in the first place.

Narcissists are driven by selfish motivations to increase their status and seek validation in people's eyes. When they get into a relationship with someone, they realize that the person they are with isn't perfect, so they try their hardest to change them according to their specification. When the other person protests, the narcissist breaks their character down bit by bit through manipulation and passive-aggressive techniques and achieves their goal.

A narcissist may verbally abuse, use sarcasm and threats, manipulation, emotional blackmail, gaslighting, exploiting and objectifying, giving silent treatment, and financially abusing their partner to break them. They demonize their personality, strengths, flaws, decisions, mentality, point-of-view, and way of living. This can make the victim lose their sense of reality as they're constantly plagued by doubt in themselves, their actions, their decisions, and their thoughts. They become an extension of the narcissist's will, and this immersion destroys them entirely because they become a slave to the narcissist's needs and wants. This is why when they're released from this constricting relationship, they walk about like a man senseless, unknowing how to behave in the outside world when their inner world is in such turmoil.

SIGNS AND SYMPTOMS OF NAS

1. They seemed so perfect — at first

During the love-bombing phase, also called chasing the unicorn phase, The narcissist would portray themselves as the most brilliant, kind, lovely, fabulous, and generous person around. They would prove to be incredibly helpful to their partner—someone who would make them feel loved and adored.

Narcissists rejoice when their victim shares their insecurities, wounds, struggles, and triggers with them—mainly because getting this information makes it easy for the narcissist to manipulate the victim. The love-bombing stage continues until the victim is entirely dependent on the narcissist and shares everything with them. The victim now trusts the narcissist unequivocally.

As an honoree of this trust, at first, the narcissist will pretend to support, be kind towards, love, and empathize with their victim, but soon this fake goodwill will vanish like so much smoke. The narcissist will begin demeaning and degrading you because they now know that you are beneath them; they know all your secrets, so they feel superior and vital—while you ,they think, to be worthless. At this stage, they will do the worst they can for you. They will hurt you as much as they can.

If you have been through something like this, then be very vigilant. You may have been a victim of a narcissist—someone who tried their hardest to destroy you. If you think your answer is in the affirmative, then try to seek therapy or talk to a friend about what you've been through.

2. People doubt the abuse took place

Narcissists are subtle and sneaky creatures; they are good at manipulation and exploitation. They leverage their charm, charisma, and seemingly good nature against any vitriol someone would spew about them. They always behave in a good-natured manner with other people while behaving the opposite way with those closest to them. So, when someone who the narcissist has damaged reveals what they've been through in their relationship, the narcissist usually acts all injured and declares that their accuser is either touched in the head or lying. People believe the narcissist because they are blinded by the narcissist's shiny exterior and, alas, know no better.

Even the victim can be unsure of what happened to them. They may believe that it was their fault that their partner was behaving atrociously. They might feel guilty for mistakes they never even made in the first place. When they remember the bouts of aggressive behavior and the silent treatment at the tiniest of issues, they may doubt their memory because people won't believe them.

3. They've started a smear campaign

Narcissists care far more for their image than they do for flesh and blood people. Their excessive need for admiration and adoration has reinforced their good impression in people's eyes constantly.

Thus, if you've wised up to the tricks the narcissists employ to manipulate and exploit you, telling people about them will get you nothing. The narcissist's image is too firmly rooted in the minds of people. If you try to tell your loved ones what happened to you, they may not believe you. Similarly, you would get the same response from your friends because they believe the image that the narcissist represents.

Also, when you start trying to discredit the narcissist's image and expose their lies, they may retaliate with extreme prejudice. If you use harsh language against them—exposing their lies and abuse, they may twist your words into something you had never meant. Where you try to expose the lies, they may brand you the liar. You try to recount your experiences. They may shut you up by branding you crazy or jealous, or sulky.

4. You feel isolated

When no one listens to you, loneliness takes place in your heart. The narcissist has successfully isolated you from people. Those who once thought you intelligent, coherent, and clear now feel about you as an incoherent, envious, and hollowed-out person. The narcissist's image is too strong to break, no matter how hard you try.

You may start to doubt yourself, going as far as to think that the abuse didn't happen. When people are alone and have no one to talk to, things and events become unrealistic to them. They may find themselves in a fugue—thinking that whatever happened to them was not real. Experiences and memories become dull due to the wealth of loneliness and despair until finally, the victim may become desperate to connect with anyone—even their abusers. All just to get a little bit of human interaction.

5. You freeze-up

Abuse leaves its victims scarred—some more and others less. Emotional abuse leaves more scars than physical abuse ever because the impacts of emotional wounds are severe and devastating to the victim throughout their lives. Some people get scared of being alone with people; others may not even meet the eyes of their friends, family, or colleagues because they feel too ashamed at what happened to them. Still, others may freeze or stop like statues when they feel helpless.

This freeze response is not just limited to physical acts. Instead, it is linked to emotional distancing too. People who have been through narcissistic abuse may try to numb their emotions to function in life. They may mute their personality or cut aspects of their character because they don't know how to live among people anymore. When these people find themselves in a difficult situation, they may not defend themselves because they are paralyzed with fear.

6. You have trouble making decisions

The constant devaluation and degradation exhibited by a narcissistic partner can leave the victim unable to trust themselves. The cutting remarks, cruel observations, cold looks, and callous misinterpretations of your behavior can make the victim incur a massive blow to their self-esteem. Due to the narcissist's constant abuse, the victims may think that they cannot make the right decisions because they don't have the requisite qualities to do so.

So, when an abusive partner tells you, "Love, I have never seen someone more stupid than you are. Why did you even do this without my help?" you, as the person who has been abused, thinks nothing of the lies and believes, straightaway, that you're the one at fault. Narcissists often use these techniques to make their victims dependent on them—mainly because they want their victims to suffer as much as possible. They want their solid and confident partner to become flaky and constantly second-guess themselves.

7. You always feel like you've done something wrong

No matter what you do, your partner is never appreciative of your actions. He constantly degrades your actions and words, calls you naive and unintelligent, and gets angry at you when you pay him no attention. You always feel like you've done something wrong, even if you think you did all you could.

Narcissists are masters at making people feel this way. Since they believe that people are extensions of themselves and are there for fulfilling their needs, narcissists treat those closest to them atrociously. They project their needs over others, thinking that what they need is much more important than others' needs. So, when you do something that doesn't benefit them, they act out and make you feel as if you're the one who is doing wrong, not them.

If you find that they've lied to you about something important, they may tell you disparagingly and condescendingly that you wouldn't understand or that you would've reacted terribly if you'd known. They may even get angry at you for trying to accuse them, often accusing you back of something they themselves did to you. They may rant and rave about the sacrifices they'd done for you, only to be treated this way. This outlandish behavior may leave you emotionally crippled,-making you think that you are always wrong no matter what you do.

8. You have unexplained physical symptoms

Abuse can be both emotionally and physically devastating. After getting out of their relationship, some people can suffer from crippling anxiety and low self-esteem. These feelings can exhibit physical symptoms such as flashbacks, lack of appetite, gastrointestinal issues, muscle aches and pains, constant fatigue, insomnia, and nightmares about their experiences.

9. You feel restless and unsettled

People with narcissistic personality disorder are pathologically volatile. Their self-esteem changes from day to day, so their behavior becomes unpredictable. One day, they may be the most loving of spouses, reciprocating your love and affection, while on other days, even if you're being kind and paying them their due attention, they may be harsh, demeaning, and degrading.

This constant back and forth can drive you up the wall. Frustration, anxiety, and tension become your constant bedmates. You are always alert to every word and action your partner says or performs. You feel that you can't let your guard down because if you did, you may be blindsided by something you could've seen before. You are always tense, expecting a backlash to something you didn't even do in the first place. This tension can leave you unable to relax and feel calm, often causing harmful effects on your body and your psyche.

10. You don't recognize yourself

People with narcissism manipulate and exploit their partners. By using belittling language, they make you acquiesce to their demands. They were using sweet-nothings. They prompt you to deviate from your desired course. Day-by-day, under the ministrations of the narcissist, you lose a part of yourself—a part of who you used to be. The narcissist forges you into the thing they want you to be—a subservient, dependent, and unopinionated creature who is less than human.

Narcissists hold no regard for anyone but themselves; they are self-centered. This belief prompts them to take actions that no person with moral obligations would consider.

They don't stop from using any weapon to make you less. So, when they're done with their updates, you may be a lesser version of yourself. You may become purposeless, cut adrift, and depend on your partner for everything—someone who cannot appreciate or enjoy life as it is and used to be.

11. You have trouble setting boundaries

At the start of the relationship, narcissists encourage you to share everything about yourself with them. When you do, they take this information and manipulate you into doing things for them—something they cannot do for themselves. When some of these things or actions cross the boundaries or tenants you've set up for yourself, you may object to the narcissist's orders and protest against them. Since narcissists are fickle, they may ignore your outrage, blame everything on you, or challenge you to make them adhere to your boundaries.

When victims reinforce their boundaries, the narcissist may not even pay any attention to them. Even if the victim tries to enforce their demands, the narcissist—who is canny, charismatic, and charming—cajoles and wheedles back into the good graces of the victim. Eventually, the victim—seeing that there is no point in setting down boundaries—will stop reinforcing their choices altogether.

12. You have symptoms of anxiety and depression

Anxiety and depression are expected consequences of narcissistic abuse. When a narcissist constantly degrades and demeans their partner, their confidence in themselves and their self-esteem is shattered. They believe that they are not worth anything and are filled with immense self-doubt, leading to depression.

The victim may feel hopeless, hollow, or empty after they've suffered through the abuse. Things that once brought them joy only remind them of the misery they suffered through. When the victim doesn't know that their partner was a narcissist, they may believe that what happened to them was a consequence of their actions. This belief may result in self-loathing, which may emotionally imbalance the victim and lead them into a dark depression.

13. You experience relationship amnesia after the relationship ends

People who suffer through narcissistic relationships often think that they never had good relationships. They recall the abusive behavior of their narcissistic partner and can't remember anything before that. They have been traumatized so much that they have no recall of those people who were good to them before this relationship.

THE THREE-STAGE PATTERN OF ABUSE

It is crucial that we learn—in any relationship—to identify the red flags when interacting with people who display malignant narcissistic traits or have been diagnosed with NPD. To protect ourselves from abuse and exploitation, set appropriate boundaries, and make informed decisions about who we keep in our lives. Understanding how narcissists operate and how they affect their victims can help us identify the red flags easily when such people target us.

Narcissists can target anyone. Their victims can be of any gender, age, background, and socioeconomic status. Often the victims are so blinded by the charming and charismatic persona shown by the narcissist that they forget to look that underneath all the glitter resides a core so malicious and rotten that nothing compares to it.

1. Chasing the Unicorn/love-bombing/Idealization Phase.

Of the three stages of narcissistic abuse, chasing the unicorn—also known as "love-bombing" and "the idealization phase"—is the most disarming.

In the love bombing stage—very aptly named—the narcissist tries his best to charm the object of their affection and make them dependent on him. Some people describe this stage as the most "magical" and "beautiful" and "wonderous" state of their life. For many, this is the first time they've been regarded with such affection, fondness, and love. The narcissist tries his utmost best to target emotionally vibrant people, have good status, are loved and respected, and are good people overall because their adulation from being with these well-regarded people is as addictive as a shot of cocaine.

Once they catch these people, they put them on a pedestal, lavish them with affection and love, make them the center of their world, and shower them with flattery and praise. They convince their partner that they are their soulmate. The mirror mimics the partner's values, hobbies, interests, thought patterns, and feelings to manufacture this "soulmate" effect. At times, narcissists may even pay excessive attention to their partner to manipulate them. This can be shown through constant texting, shallow flattery, and the need to be around you all the time. This "love-bombing" sucks in people like fleas. They are flattered and disarmed by the (apparently) sincere attention. They may even be fooled into thinking that the narcissist is genuinely interested in them when the narcissist is only interested in making their partner dependent on their constant love and attention.

This phase is also the most dangerous because the narcissist collects all the insecurities, flaws, and shortcomings you've confided in them as weapons that they'd later use on you. They wheedle into your graces and have you share your wounds, struggles, and triggers with them. This makes it much easier for them to get under your skin later on in the relationship. After all, the constant love, praise, and admiration are heady, and it makes you feel trusting and open with your partner—who you think loves you as you are—but is instead just collecting enough ammunition to destroy you. Due to this, you share everything with them: your past, your heartbreaks, and what you perceive to be your flaws with them, seeing this as a way to establish rapport—a connection to show them that you understand them and a way to get closer to them. On the other hand, the narcissist sees this as prey laying itself down on the dinner table on its own, and noticing this, starts to sharpen its teeth in anticipation of the kill.

2. Construction Project

After the idealization phase, the construction project phase is the phase where the narcissist abruptly pushes you of the pedestal they established in the first phase. They start to suggest improvements you could make in your character, emotions, feelings, thinking patterns, behavior, skill, and social circle.

You will become irritating to the narcissist because you have become dependent on the narcissist's constant praise and admiration. The narcissist may then start backing away, blowing hot one second and cold the next. Their flattering and affectionate glances may become as hard as a glacier. Their loving gestures may turn into taunts aimed at your body, and their flowery words, full of praise for you, may become as barren as a desert. They may turn away from you, leaving you confused and lost, wondering what you did that made the narcissist back away.

3. Devaluation

In this last stage, the abuse starts. The narcissist begins to question their partner's behavior, making a problem out of every aspect of their personality. They begin to treat their partner as objects, play with them, and put them down whenever they feel like it.

When the partner questions the narcissist's sudden withdrawal, the narcissist may be prompted into a rage—called narcissistic rage. They may become angry at the suggestion that they aren't worth listening to. Ordinary people would understand their partner's view. They would understand that every person has the right to choose and that this right cannot be taken away from them by anyone. Narcissists do not recognize people's autonomy in the first place, so they cannot be expected to imagine that people have values and beliefs different from the— values and beliefs unrelated to the narcissist's well-being. Narcissists cannot comprehend that anyone could be better than them; they can't believe that there is someone in the world who would try not to meet their unreasonable demands, which is why, in the end, they start to become abusive towards their partner.

The narcissist devalues, invalidates, gaslights, and emotionally blackmails their partner into teaching them a lesson. Narcissists are skilled manipulators, and they use this skill to bring their partner down to their knees. They sabotage their partner's relationships with others, objectify them, withhold money, communication, sex, or affection from them, and neglect their needs to teach them a lesson.

The flaws, insecurities, heartbreaks, wounds, struggles, and triggers the partner shared with the narcissist in the "love-bombing" stage will now be used to provoke, belittle, and demean the partner. If the partner had been abused in the past, the narcissist would not hesitate to use the memory of abuse to objectify and cause them harm. They use every tool in their possession, no matter how horrible, to get a reaction from their partner, and it is this irreverent usage of personal facts that finally breaks the partner into pieces. They had trusted the narcissist with the secret of who they were, and they got only abuse in return.

WHAT THE VICTIM GOES THROUGH

Victims often experience:

1. Fear and anxiety

Due to the narcissist's constant polar behavior, their partner is always on their toes, always ready for something to happen. At one moment, the narcissist can be incredibly gentle and full of kindness. At the same time, on the other, they can be exceedingly hurtful and malicious.

This behavioral polarity drives the partner to become anxious and fearful of the narcissist; they become afraid of the narcissist's unpredictable behavior because they don't know what they will get when they talk to them. The constant cutting remarks and verbal abuse also play a massive role in driving the partner to become fearful of the narcissist.

2. That they are the cause of the problem

Through the love-bombing phase, the narcissist constantly extols the virtues of their partner and puts them on a pedestal. They make the object of their desire feel like the most beautiful, appreciated and loved person in the world until they become dependent on the narcissist's praise and admiration.

When a narcissist realizes that their partner has become dependent on them, they become scathing, verbally abusive, and cruel towards them. The narcissist tells their partner that he/she is not giving their all to them—that he/she could become even better if she/she listens to the narcissist. If the partner does listen, then the narcissist becomes accommodating and kind, but then the narcissist becomes incredibly cruel if the partner doesn't. This polarity cements into the partner's mind that all that is happening to them is their fault. They think that if they could be just a little better, the narcissist would love them.

3. Mood swings

Living with a narcissist is traumatic. The people who suffer through this abuse often become volatile. The narcissist treats them like a prize hound—favoring them when they obey and whipping them when they disobey. This constant back-and-forth rewrites the emotional and psychological patterns of the victim—the victim becomes more prone who lashing out because of their pain and getting depressed due to the bleakness of their life, all of which renders them unable to function at times.

4. Deterioration of their self-image and self-esteem

The constant degrading, demeaning, and cruel comments issued by the narcissist on their victim's behavior, intelligence, thinking patterns, body, cooking skills, health, flaws, strengths, hurts and wounds, and appearance can cause the victim to lose their sense of self—which leads to the deterioration of their confidence and self-esteem. Every abusive word is like a knife into their heart—every cruel action gives them pain.

At first, the narcissist may be cross about a few things, such as the victim's appearance. Still, over time, the strengths that the narcissist once praised become "flaws," intelligence becomes "pride," and confidence becomes "belligerence." Every positive quality is twisted into a negative rate until no victim aspect is positive anymore. The constant abuse whittles away the victim's self-esteem until they become dependent on the narcissist for approving comments so they can feel, for just a while, that they're worth it.

5. Unable to break away

The regular abuse changes the victim's perception—some victims may even, in fact, fall in love with their abuser and bond with them, leaving them unable to walk away from them. The victims may feel that nobody would appreciate them more than their partner and not live without the narcissist.

This dependence on the appreciation or understanding of the narcissist can take a heavy toll on the victim's psyche. Due to their convictions, the victim may become unable to walk away from their partner, even when they realize that their partner is abusive towards them. Even knowing the depth of the errors committed by their partner towards them, the victims may still stay with their partner because they know no better anymore.

6. Intense loneliness

When your partner appreciates nothing you do, you start to feel overlooked. All the beautiful dinners you made, the lovely friends you gave them, or your money at their disposal means nothing to them. When you try to love them, they take that love and return nothing. When you try to talk to your friends and family about your partner's behavior, they are full of disbelief and think you are crazy. In all these instances, you may experience intense loneliness. Your partner doesn't appreciate you or your gifts, and your family and friends don't believe you —your life is without any meaningful interaction.

People in narcissistic relationships often feel overlooked and lonely, mainly because the narcissist takes all their attention and reciprocates nothing at all. All relationships are built based on give-and-take, and when this doesn't happen, problems arise. When one partner doesn't appreciate or ignores the other, they inevitably cause them to feel lonely and lost, unable to find the love they wanted and needed.

7. Being gaslighted

Also called brainwashing, gaslighting is a tactic employed by many narcissists to alter and convince their partner to change their perception. Narcissists intentionally make their partner distrust their view of reality or make them believe that they're mentally unstable. Often, victims who are gaslighted believe that they are no longer the person they used to be, that everything wrong is their fault, that they are the problem in the relationship, and much more.

Gaslighting can be done by a narcissist towards anyone close or dear to them, such as their spouse, friends, family, colleagues, and fellow workers. It is always underhanded and causes changes in a person's emotional and psychological thinking patterns. It can also cause severe emotional and psychological trauma to the victim—which can be very dangerous to their survival.

8. Feelings of inadequacy

Narcissists are very charming and charismatic people. When they seduce someone during the love-bombing phase, they make that person dependent on the praise, admiration, and love given by them. Therefore, when the narcissist becomes demeaning towards their beloved, they make their beloved feel that they're inadequate.

Narcissists take everything from the object of their attention and give nothing back. When something doesn't meet their specifications, they become wrathful, and when something does, they become kind and gentle. This polarity produces feelings of inadequacy in the hearts of the victims. The victims start to believe that no matter how much they love, goodwill, and attention to give to the narcissist, they will never be enough for them.

9. That the relationship engulfs them

Narcissists are self-centered and seek everything for themselves. This self-importance can cause the victim to feel that their voice is never heard in the relationship, that only the needs and wants of the narcissist are essential.

As the abuse continues, this realization becomes concrete. The victim gives everything to their abuser, and yet, the abuser still wants more. They want everything—even the things their victim cannot provide them. Therefore, in a relationship with a grandiose narcissist, the victim becomes an accessory to the narcissist's needs and nothing more.

10. That their integrity and values are compromised

Abuse can change the perception of the victim. Due to the constant devaluation done by narcissists, they may do things that they never wanted or believed they could do. If the narcissists ask them to do something, they may please the narcissist even if they think the action is deplorable or horrifying.

Thus, in a narcissistic relationship, the narcissists break down their victim's values and integrity until they become no more than a puppet who fulfills their needs.

11. Name-calling

The narcissist's excessive need for admiration and arrogance leaves them emotionally vulnerable. They want to believe that they are the best, most perfect, and the most lovely, intelligent, or kind person around.

This is why, when a narcissist is slapped in the face with their lack of achievement, accomplishment, charisma, or is accused of imperfection, the narcissist lashes out at their partner with anger and rage. They project their faults onto their partners, objectify them, label them, call them names, and behave atrociously towards them.

The name-calling, at such times, can be particularly severe as the narcissist uses all the secrets, hurts, and flaws they discovered about their victim to try to destroy them.

12. Constant cycles of pain and joy

Narcissists are volatile. A narcissist can be both hot and cold at once in a relationship. They may be sadistic, cruel, and abusive when their partner does or say something they don't like, while at other times when they appreciate what the partner did for them, they may be gentle, loving, and kind.

This constant cycle goes round and round until it is stopped. If the narcissist demands something and the victim disagrees, they may become cold and harsh. They are seeing this harshness, the victim consents. The narcissist, seeing the submission, becomes kind. Most of the time, the constant polarity changes the tenants and beliefs of the victim, usually making them believe that they can't live without their partner. At other times, this polarity can also drive a person to depression and even death because they feel inadequate to fulfill their partner's needs.

TRAUMA BONDING: A CYCLE YOU CAN'T ESCAPE

What Is Trauma?

In essence, trauma is an emotional response to a deeply distressing or disturbing event that threatens an individual's sense of safety or security and overwhelms their ability to cope with the event. It can also cause a person to feel isolated, diminishes their sense of self, and leaves them unable to feel the full range of their emotions and experiences. Therefore, a traumatic event causes physical, emotional, and psychological harm.

Living with a person with narcissistic tendencies can be traumatic as they can almost casually hurt their partner. Narcissists are self-centered and think of others as meaningless—that other people's needs and wants are negligible. In a relationship, this selfishness causes much harm. The narcissist verbally abuses, emotionally blackmail, gaslight, or brainwashing, and invades their partner's privacy to get what he wants.

Relationships with narcissists are unpredictable. This is mainly because narcissists have a pathological need for admiration to regulate their low and fluctuating self-esteem. When they don't get that admiration, they lash out at others with extreme prejudice, often causing them excessive harm in the process. The most severe effect of this unpredictability is that the partner never knows where they stand with the narcissist. One minute the narcissist could be as charming as a sweet child, and the next, he could be as venomous as a snake. These constant highs and lows make it hard for the partner to feel safe in the relationship, which causes them immense trauma.

How Does Trauma Bonding With a Narcissist Happen?

In this case, the term "trauma bonding" refers to the relationship that develops between the abuser and the victim over a long period of exposure to each other. However, it can also refer to a reasonable bond that develops between two people, one of whom shares their experience with the other to alleviate their tension.

In a narcissistic relationship, trauma bonding forms through a cycle of abuse and idealization. The narcissist abuses their partner, demeans and discredits them, belittles and gaslights them, and then discards them like trash. Still, after a while, the narcissist goes back to their victim, or their victim goes back to the narcissist, and the cycle begins anew.

To go into further detail, when a narcissist gets into a relationship with someone else, they change the paradigms their partner holds—they manipulate their partner into changing their worldview and make them perceive a different meaning of intimacy than they previously had. This altered perception or intermittent reinforcement causes immense problems. First of all, even after getting out of the relationship, the victim may not be able to live without the particular brand of affection given to them by their abuser.

Secondly, the polarity in behavior displayed by the narcissist leaves victims confused. At one moment, the narcissist is hot with rage, and the next, they're affectionate and kind. People who have yearned for attention all their lives can become desperate for attention, so when a narcissist gives them that attention, they become addicted to it. Similarly, when the narcissist is through with the love-bombing phase, they leave their victim addicted to their affection, kindness, and praise. This addiction causes problems, which is why the result is terrible for the victim in both scenarios. Since the victim displays an overt vulnerability, the narcissist tries their hardest to exploit that chink in the victim's armor to make them further dependent on them.

Over time, this relationship can become customary for the victim and the abuser. The victim upheld the values, beliefs, and tenants when they first began the relationship unravels and mutates into something new. This change of perception is often comparable to "Stockholm syndrome," which is a psychological response that abuse victims exhibit when they bond with their abusers. In the case of a narcissistic relationship, the victim becomes enamored of their lover and turns themselves inside out to meet the needs of their abuser.

You feel stuck

Victims who have bonded with their abusers often feel a sense of twisted obligation, affection, or love for their abuser—the trauma may create these feelings. After all, it is only natural to love someone for their kindness, and narcissists are kind in spades, at least at first. However, while generating feelings, the constant abuse also twists the perception of the victim. Since their perception of personal behavior has been changed by the actions of their abuser, they become predisposed to such conduct and take it up as the new norm. They lose their sense of self in the process, which means that they lose their autonomy over themselves and become an extension of their abuser—a resource which the narcissist uses as he sees fit.

Traumatized people need support and time to recover from the traumatic event. Still, when the trauma is piled into previous trauma, the victim becomes used to the abuse and cannot break away from their abuser.

However, if the victim does realize that they have to get out of this abusive relationship, they may find that people do not support or help them through their ordeal. This is mainly because people cannot see the trauma the victims have been through—they don't know the depth of their indecisiveness and inability to make decisions. Sometimes people may not even believe the victims, prompting them to go back to what is safe rather than try to do something new and scary.

Suggesting that "Just leave them!" doesn't cut it. There is a wealth of understanding needed to prompt abuse victims to walk away from their abusive partners. Most of the time, if a victim realizes how much worse their relationship is, they need backup to get out of it. If they don't get this back up through the support of other people, they may find that they feel stuck, giving them no option but to go back to their abuser.

SIGNS OF TRAUMA BONDING WITH A NARCISSIST

Trauma bonds can have some visible and some not-so-visible signs because sometimes the changes that abuse incites can be done deep in the victim's psyche.

Common signs of traumatic bonding with a narcissist that a victim display are:

1. You feel unhappy about the relationship but cannot break it because of false attachment.
2. When you enforce your boundaries, your partner promises to change, but they never do. Yet, you still stay with them.
3. If you try to leave the narcissist, you feel physically or emotionally distressed.
4. You think about the "good" days of your relationship to convince yourself that your narcissistic partner does care about you.
5. You excuse and defend the narcissist's abusive behavior to yourself and others.
6. You continue to trust your partner and hope that they will change when all evidence points to the contrary.
7. They have all the power in the relationship, so they control you to the point that you can no longer resist or know how to break free.
8. You feel incomplete and lost without your partner; you feel like they give you life.
9. You constantly forgive your partner for their abuse and go back to them again and again.
10. If you do leave them, you may be having a hard time living without them because you've become dependent on them.

Trauma bonds can cast long shadows even after the end of the relationship and a lot of therapy. Victims usually struggle to stop thinking about their abuser and the hurts and wounds they gave to them. If you feel you have bonded with your abuser, ask yourself this question: If you saw someone you love going through the same abusive relationship you are going through, would you ask them to end it?

If you answered in the affirmative but still feel incredibly powerless to leave your relationship, then that's a sure-fire sign of trauma bonding.

4

LONG-TERM EFFECTS OF NARCISSISTIC ABUSE

WHAT THE VICTIM FEELS AND THINKS ABOUT HERSELF, HER LIFE, AND THE NARCISSIST?

Living in a relationship with a narcissist is traumatic. A narcissist thinks that they are the only one in the relationship entitled to have their needs fulfilled. Their self-centeredness makes it impossible for them to look out from under their rock and realize that other people also have needs. Malicious narcissists, in particular, feed on other people's pain, which they cause through various means until they control their victim's desires, thoughts, and actions.

Over years of abuse, the victim develops scars that are difficult to heal. The constant critical analysis offered by the narcissist can make the victim feel like that it's their fault that everything is wrong with their relationship. In reality, this is not true at all. The narcissist silences their victims' needs and feelings and leaves them unable to thrive. Narcissists make sure that their victim knows that only the narcissist can help them survive because they are superior and know better. They force their victims into compliance and conformity and leave them unable to make their own decisions.

Over months or years of abuse, a victim's mind is often focused on getting an explanation for the different ways they make the narcissist treat them horribly. They believe that everything that happened to them was their fault, and so, they try to justify everything the narcissist does to them to themselves.

The narcissist makes the victim dependent on them, leaving them unable to do as they will. The victim, as a result, feels that nobody is as helpful or as understanding as their narcissistic partner. They trust their partner to take care of them because nobody else does or will.

The victim thinks the world of their partner, even after being abused constantly. They take any attention, even negative attention, as a sign of affection and care and think that their partner only wants the best for them.

EFFECTS OF LONG-TERM RELATIONSHIPS WITH NARCISSISTS

Anyone who has been in a relationship with a narcissist can attest that narcissists are self-centered people who often abuse their partner to get what they want. Usually, this abuse—sarcastic remarks, critical analyses, cutting, and cruel glances, and unfair comparisons—can result in emotional and psychological trauma that the victim usually bears. In their attempts at manipulating, exploiting, gaslighting, brainwashing, and victimizing their partner, the narcissist can cross boundaries and break trusts that cause immense pain.

The breakage of these trusts and boundaries can cause the victim to incur trauma, limiting their social mobility. According to mental health experts, often, people victimized by narcissists develop C-PTSD—a complex form of post-traumatic stress disorder that leaves the victims unable to lead happy and fulfilling lives. C-PTSD is linked to prolonged abuse and is, therefore, suffered by people who narcissists have abused for a very long time.

CHARACTERISTICS OF C-PTSD

PTSD is a disorder diagnosed when a person undergoes a single traumatic event. Complex PTSD, on the other hand, is only diagnosed if a person has experienced prolonged or recurring trauma over a long duration—over a few months or years—or on an ongoing basis. C-PTSD can be caused by childhood neglect; sexual, emotional, or physical abuse in childhood or adulthood; domestic abuse; oppression, and slavery.

People with C-PTSD often have very negative self-conceptions —characterized by self-doubt and self-loathing. Often, people with this disorder can feel that they are the problem in a relationship; they think they're always wrong and never do anything right. They may have skewed perceptions of reality after going through the abuse and may develop xenophobic tendencies against their abusers and their ilk. For example, a child who a narcissist abuses may grow up unable to trust others because he thinks that others would only use him for their purpose.

Like all mental disorders, C-PTSD also has several unique characteristics. People who are diagnosed with C-PTSD display:

1. A high level of disassociation from the abuse they've undergone: Someone who has been abused may back away or try their hardest to detach themselves from feeling the trauma they've undergone.

2. Difficulties in regulating their emotions: Abuse victims may find it hard to stay calm. They may experience crippling fear, panic attacks, nightmares, and flashbacks of the abuse they'd suffered due to their lack of control.

3. A negative self-conception: People with C-PTSD may think negatively and may feel ashamed or guilty. They may believe that they were the problem in the relationship and can, as a result, become wrought with self-loathing.

4. Relationship issues: Abuse engenders trust issues. So, people who have been through prolonged abuse do not trust others. Furthermore, abuse also reduces the social mobility of abuse victims. Therefore, a person who has such issues may not create and facilitate healthy relationships.

5. Fixation on an abuser: Someone who has been abused may become preoccupied with their abuser, especially the relationship and the abuse they had with the abuser. They may also entertain fantasies of getting revenge on the abuser.

6. Changes in perception: Abuse changes the perception and outlook of an individual. Some victims might lose their faith or have beliefs proven wrong. Others may develop a more cynical outlook on life and people. Still, others might find that they have created anathema qualities to them once.

HOW CAN EMOTIONAL TRAUMA CAUSE PTSD?

PTSD is a mental disorder or condition in people who have gone through or witnessed a single traumatic event that was frightening, distressing, or horrifying and stopped them from living their lives correctly. Once associated with physical causes like war, physical assault, and sexual assault, PTSD has been linked to emotional trauma by a multitude of mental health experts. The form of PTSD caused by emotional trauma is called C-PTSD, which is usually a response to prolonged ongoing trauma borne by an individual with an inability to leave the situation.

Emotional trauma is caused when one person manipulates another to get what they want. This manipulation can include gaslighting, verbal abuse, objectification, exploitation, invasion of privacy, and projection, among others.

In the case of a narcissistic relationship, the victim suffers immense emotional trauma at the hands of her abuser. A narcissist may take the victim's freedom, invade her privacy, and verbally abuse her to get what they want. This abuse can have adverse effects on the victim and cause them to develop C-PTSD with symptoms ranging from distress, loss of sense of self, and lack of emotional regulation to severe depression.

Many victims who suffer from C-PTSD caused by narcissistic relationships claim that they feel insane, question themselves, don't trust anyone close to them, have lost their self-control, feel ashamed or insecure of themselves, are filled with self-doubt and self-loathing, and have become very cynical after going through the trauma.

SYMPTOMS OF C-PTSD

1. Intrusive, invasive, or otherwise unwanted thoughts
2. Triggers—physical or emotional responses to situations that are similar or reminiscent of traumatic situations
3. Flashbacks and nightmares—recurring instances in which the individual feels like they're reliving a traumatic experience
4. Avoiding people, places, or situations associated with the narcissistic individual
5. Feeling isolated, alone, or detached from others
6. Feeling extremely alert or vigilant all the time—unable to sleep, lack of concentration, emotional volatility.
7. Loss of trust in both themselves and others
8. Insomnia—difficulty sleeping

SYMPTOMS OF PTSD AND NARCISSISTIC ABUSE SYNDROME

Emotional and physical abuse, both of which often cause PTSD, have several symptoms that are very similar to the symptoms of narcissistic abuse syndrome. This mental disorder occurs when an individual suffers from abuse perpetrated by a narcissist an individual with a narcissistic personality disorder.

1. Feeling stuck and confused.
2. Having nightmares or flashbacks.
3. High level of hyperarousal; anxiety, nervousness, jumpy, obsessive thinking, racing thoughts, feeling scared, agitated, stressed, overwhelmed, emotional, etc.
4. Overreacting
5. Difficulties controlling emotions
6. Numbing your emotions
7. Imagining "worst-case" scenarios
8. Being on the edge
9. Guilt/Shame
10. Feeling numb/zoning out/disconnectedness/dissociation
11. Fatigue and extreme tiredness.
12. Physical manifestation of trauma and abuse
13. Unhealthy coping strategies
14. Suicidal thoughts/fantasies

LONG TERM EFFECTS ON THE CHILDREN OF A NARCISSIST PARENT

The effects of abuse on a child are much more profound than those on adults. Children acquiesce to abusive behavior because they bow to the authority of those older than them. Many times, children know no better. The same parent who may be a saint in public can be a devil in private. They may be the perfect parent out in public, but in private, they may be the parent who rages, manipulates, exploits, and gaslights their children. This subtle abuse can cause many harmful effects on the child both emotionally and psychologically.

If children have experienced narcissistic abuse in their childhood, they may suffer from a few or all of the following symptoms.

1. Neediness: Children of narcissistic parents often learn to fit into the molds their parents create for them. Their parents often treat them harshly because they fail to meet their parent's expectations, even if the fault lies at the parent's end. This manipulation and exploitation result in the child becoming starved for true love, kindness, and affection—things that they never get from their parent. In adult life, this need becomes debilitating because it can make these children see affection or love where it wasn't meant to be. At other times, due to the lack of emotional fulfillment in their childhood, these children are exposed to "love-bombing"—the tactic narcissists employ to make their victims dependent on them.

2. Self-Criticism: Children with narcissistic parents learn early on to blame themselves for everything that goes wrong in their lives. This is mainly because the narcissistic parent projects their needs over their children and makes sure that the child is only there to fulfill their needs. When those needs aren't fulfilled—maybe the child was too young, perhaps the child couldn't cook, couldn't clean properly, or write correctly—the narcissist parent lashes out at their children, causing them immense emotional and psychological harm. Children who go through such trauma think that whatever happened is their fault—that their parent is correct and that they're incompetent at whatever they do. This belief can destroy relationships and limit success because the child doesn't have the confidence to stand up and do what they want—they think that they are the worst of the worst—and it can also translate into self-loathing at the actions they were forced to do by their parents.

3. Insecure Attachment: Narcissistic parents project their own needs over the needs of their children—their children are only present over there to fulfill their needs. As a result, due to this self-interest, narcissistic parents ignore their children's emotional and physical needs—they do not provide the child with the proper amount of care and appreciation the child needs and can, at times, even neglect the needs and wants of the child entirely. Their child completely trusts them, but they don't reciprocate this trust at all, punishing them at the slightest of offenses—whether true or not. This emotional and physical neglect stresses upon the child that they can't trust their parent to do good by them, that nobody will ever do good by them if they are vulnerable. And to avoid being vulnerable, these children either avoid forming relationships entirely or become emotionally detached in relationships—unwittingly causing the same harm to others that were done to them.

4. Shrinking: Narcissistic parents tend to see their children as an extension of themselves, a source of self-esteem for the parent. The child becomes a receptacle of admiration for the narcissistic parent, and to get this praise from other people, narcissists do anything they can to get it. They may make the child adhere to their agenda and assert their feelings and thoughts over them, which can often lead to problems when the child doesn't perform as well as the parent wanted them to. The parent then punishes the child for every wrong committed, even wrongs committed by the parent. In later life, this abuse can show itself as an inability to face anything. People who have suffered from such abuse try to fade into the background because they have learned that attracting the attention of anybody can be harmful.

5. Sensitivity: In this case, children who have been abused by narcissistic parents can become both emotionally volatile or highly competent at managing their emotions. Since these children had to address the needs of their parents at such a young age, they become receptive to the emotional variances of their parents. Some children can even observe how their parents manipulate others and learn to spot that manipulation when used on themselves; however, this is very rare as rarely do children possess the level of self-awareness required to do this. In most cases, children become highly emotionally volatile and can in their later life be very aggressive, even xenophobic, towards those who abused them.

6. Physical symptoms: Increased rates of eating disorders, substance abuse, obesity, heart disease, and mental health problems, in general, have all been linked to emotional abuse in childhood. This is mainly because child abuse causes immense distress to the child that often flows out into their future life. The effects of this abuse can hamper their efforts to live an everyday life and can drive these emotionally abused children to commit substance abuse. Some children focus on food, alcohol, and drugs to ward away their memories, flashbacks, and remembrances. Others can stop eating or taking care of themselves because they think they are worthless. Still, others may develop medical problems, such as high blood pressure, due to the stress their experience caused them throughout their life.

LONG TERM EFFECTS ON ADULTS

Adult abuse can have fewer debilitating consequences than childhood abuse can have. A child who is abused may not ever be able to function in life properly because children can't understand and change what is happening to them.

The severity of the level of abuse depends on how far the abusive individual is rated on the narcissistic personality disorder spectrum. The higher the individual is placed, the more malignant they are, and the lower they're rated, the milder they are. Malignant narcissists cause a lot of harm to the emotional psychology of the people they contact. This abuse can have both short-term and long-term effects.

Short-term effects can include:

Feelings of shame, fear, helplessness, and confusion—the victim wonders why they're being treated this way. Other times, victims also feel helpless because they can't change what is happening to them.

Unexplained aches and pains—repressed emotion can cause severe harm to the body. Repressed anger has been shown to weaken the body's muscles and damage the heart by increasing blood pressure.

Mood swings—people who have been abused lack the ability to regulate their emotions because they're controlled or stopped feeling them for far too long.

Elevated heart rate—this can be tied to a lack of emotional regulation, which makes the victim fearful or wrathful at what is happening to them.

Nightmares- can mostly be a product of remembering the abuse inflicted on the victim by the abuser.

Inability to concentrate—the victim may not focus on anything because they may be fixated on the abuse done to them by their abuser.

Long-term effects can include:

Sleep disorders such as insomnia—can happen due to nightmares, irregular hormones, and inability to sleep.

Social withdrawal or disassociation—mainly because the victim cannot bear to be with people without trusting them. Most people who have been abused develop trust issues, which hamper their social mobility.

Anxiety and depression—the victim may feel that everything is their fault and that they are "no good" because they can't do anything right.

Guilt and shame—the person may feel these emotions because of their actions under the narcissist's guidance or because they feel that they weren't able to fulfill their partner's needs.

Self-loathing or self-doubt—narcissists destroy the sense of self of their partner to make them do things they would never have thought to do before and to make them dependent on the narcissist. When a victim becomes dependent, they cannot take their own decisions and are, therefore, filled with self-doubt at every junction. They may feel self-loathing when they think about what they did for the narcissist they never wanted to do.

NARCISSIST VICTIM SYNDROME

The PTSD-like symptoms that abuse victims suffer from after they walk away from their abuser can be explained by an unofficial disorder named narcissistic victim syndrome. Simply put, narcissistic victim syndrome is a post-traumatic stress disorder that occurs when an individual suffers from abuse done to them by a person who has been diagnosed with narcissistic personality disorder (NPD). This abuse is emotional and can be done through various means such as gaslighting, manipulation, and bullying.

A person who is suffering from NVS may not keep their emotions in check. They may have intrusive, dark, and negative thoughts about themselves and their life. They may feel anxious, ashamed, and guilty about what happened to them—even going as far as to think that whatever happened to them was their fault and may have unpleasant flashbacks and nightmares of the abuse they suffered when they relax.

The effects of narcissistic abuse linger for a long time. The narcissist, to make their victim dependent on him, breaks down their sense of self to create another that is much more obedient. The changes that happen due to this breakdown aren't just emotional changes. Rather these changes affect the patterns of behavior established in the brain and, therefore, change the brain.

BRAIN DAMAGE

Narcissistic abuse has a devastating impact on an individual's emotional and psychological well-being. The emotional trauma resulting from such misuse can lead to C-PTSD—a complex form of post-traumatic stress disorder that occurs when a person undergoes abuse for an extended period of time. But, aside from disrupting the well-being of an individual and having emotional consequences, narcissistic abuse also causes changes in the brain.

Two regions of the brain, the hippocampus, and the amygdala, bear the brunt of this emotional abuse. Over time, the repeated emotional injuries caused by the narcissist shrink the hippocampus, responsible for memory and learning, while enlarging the amygdala, which is responsible for producing primitive emotions such as fear, grief, guilt, envy, and shame.

Effects on the hippocampus

The hippocampus is responsible for maintaining short-term memory and learning. Abuse affects the function of the hippocampus and causes it to shrink in size. This shrinkage is caused by the hormones that flood the brain when an individual faces an overwhelming threat. The hormones are toxic and inadvertently cause damage to the hippocampus. Dr. Douglas Bremner, in a July 1995 issue of The American Journal of Psychiatry, found out that people who had undergone childhood abuse performed at a level 40% below those who had lived an everyday and healthy life.

When the hippocampus shrinks, memory loss occurs, and learning capacity decreases. Dr. Bremner proved this by conducting an experiment in which people with post-traumatic symptoms heard a story and were then asked to repeat it 15 minutes later. Surprisingly, it was found that trauma victims had 40 percent lower accurate short-term memory than people of similar age and background.

Therefore, the shrinkage of the hippocampus, caused by cortisol—the stress hormone—when a person experiences emotional abuse, can result in short-term memory loss and reduce the learning capacity of an individual.

Effects on the amygdala

Narcissists constantly devalue and demean their victims so that they are always in a state of fear and anxiety—always in a state of readiness to anticipate their partner's needs. This constant fear and anxiety causes the victim to react from their amygdala or reptilian brain. The amygdala controls essential life functions, such as breathing, the basic emotions of fear, hate, love, and lust, and the fight and flight response that appears during times of extreme stress.

People who narcissists victimize are always in a state of readiness. They are always at the fight and flight response threshold because they have to anticipate their partner's needs before they lash out at them. Over time, as the rate of abuse increases, so does the size of this part of the brain. Even after the relationship has ended, victims can suffer from post-traumatic stress symptoms or C-PTSD or PTSD, nightmares, panic attacks, and flashbacks due to the enlargement of their amygdala.

Self-Isolation After Narcissistic Abuse

After a victim of narcissistic abuse frees herself from the clutches of the narcissist, she may expect to go back to her life, to meet those people again who used to be there for her. But this isn't easy. Often, the people who the victim neglected during the period of abuse may not want to come into contact with the victim again, isolating the victim to her misery. The victim can also refuse to contact anybody for fear of being judged or due to her anxiety and fear. The resulting depression can sap their strength and leave them unable to go out to find those who love them still.

Victims of narcissistic abuse may also distance themselves—a coping mechanism used by victims to gain control over their emotions—from everything because they may fear that they don't know how to do anything anymore. They may not be able to empathize or be socially mobile any more and may find that they do not know themselves anymore. This loss of self may prompt them to stay away from the things they previously like. They may even stay away from their family and friends to think about some way to get back into their own life.

People who have been abused may also find that they don't have any interests anymore. Everything they are was tied up in the narcissist's personality, and that after all this trauma, they don't have the sense of self they used to. They don't know what they would enjoy anymore because everything they did in the previous years or months was done to meet the needs and wants of their narcissistic partner. This lack of self-awareness may make the victim feel that they don't know themselves anymore.

This loss of sense of self happens in several different ways. In a narcissistic relationship, the abusive partner foists his opinion on his victim and makes them believe that the narcissist's opinion matters most. They use various degrading and demeaning strategies to implement this change of self. They gaslight or brainwash, exploit, manipulate, belittle, make unfair comparisons, use fear-mongering tactics, and verbally abuse their victim to get what they want. The victim, in turn, confused by the hot and cold method of treatment, tries to reconcile her views with the views of the narcissist and tries to adapt them for peace of mind. This is why people who undergo narcissistic abuse may not recognize themselves anymore.

Their Effects Last Way Long After They Are Gone

The effects of narcissistic abuse last a long time after the relationship has ended, particularly if the abuse has been going on for years. The symptoms of post-traumatic stress such as nightmares and vivid flashbacks of the traumatic moment, being fearful and easily startled; having intrusive and disturbing memories of the trauma; irritability and difficulty concentrating stay a long time after the victim has walked away from her abuser.

The effects of narcissistic abuse on children are even worse because they can lower the capabilities of a child and can tie their hands in society because they are unable to do the things their peers can do. Children can be xenophobic, have low esteem, are incapable of emotional stability, vulnerable, and can yearn for affection, which can land them in deep trouble as they can be targeted by other narcissists later in life. Some children may become aggressive due to their upbringing and may lash out at other people. Still, other children may become copies of their parents if they aren't taken out from the abusive household fast enough.

Therefore, informing yourself about narcissism, narcissistic partners, and the effects of narcissistic relationships on both you and your children can be crucial because it can help you make the active decision to walk away from your partner. Abuse should never be condoned. Anyone who abuses their partner or children is not worth being with because sometimes the abuse perpetrated by the narcissist is so harmful that it can damage regions of our brain, impair our personalities, and deplete our sense of self. This is why taking action before the action becomes impossible is vital to saving your life and your children's life.

5

HANDLING NARCISSISTIC ABUSE

HOW CAN YOU MANAGE NARCISSISTIC ABUSE?

The one thing that people with narcissistic personality disorder require is power, and in the pursuit of this goal, they diminish, degrade, and hurt other people. They try to dominate their partner into submission and try to increase their control and authority over them by shaming their partner, making them doubt themselves, and making the partner dependent on them. They don't want to appear weak, vulnerable, or shameful; they want to be the most powerful, brilliant, and lovely person in the room, and to accomplish this goal, they can do anything.

Most partners, when confronted by the narcissistic abuse behavior, may react in several different ways, of which some are:

- **Withdrawing from the argument**—The problem with this reaction is that the narcissists think they've cowed you down. They believe that you condoned their actions, which is why this isn't a **good way to deal with abuse.**
- **Pleading and Appeasement**—This tactic, again, shows weakness on your part. The narcissist realizes that you've become their groupie and will do anything to get back into their good graces. They may become condescending towards you at this point because they despise weakness, and you display it to them.
- **Fighting and getting angry**—Narcissists aren't interested in your perspective. They are incredibly self-centered and regard you as someone expendable at best. They don't care for the facts, your feelings, or your thoughts. They want to be proven right, so fighting with them is useless and serves no purpose because nothing is gained from it.
- **Giving explanations and getting defensive**—This defensive tactic gives you nothing but misery. When you start explaining your perspective, the narcissist snorts and walks away because they have no interest in hearing what you want to say. When you

define your actions or position, you give the abuser the right to judge you. They now have the power to approve and disapprove of your decisions, and more often than not, narcissists choose the latter option.

- **Criticizing and complaining**—Narcissists have extremely low self-esteem. They want to be the best. So, when you criticize them and complain about their actions, they think that their perfection is being taunted and lash out with extreme prejudice towards you. They may become vindictive and condescending towards you because you dared to hurt them.
- **Denying what happened**—If you rationalize or deny that the abuse occurred, you send the message to the narcissist that you approve of their actions and are willing to look away from anything that seems wrong to you. This action gives the narcissist more power over you because they perceive this denial as weakness, so they start exploiting you further.
- **Blaming themselves**—You are not responsible for the actions of others. You are only responsible for what you do yourself. Blaming yourself for an abuser's actions is not the best way to deal with the abuse you've suffered.

If you can't use all of the abovementioned tactics, what should you do then? The answer is that abuse should never be condoned, no matter what form it takes. Someone who abuses you is not someone you should be sharing your secrets, dreams, and hurts with.

1. Cut Them Off

Abuse damages the self-esteem of the person who is abused. This means that slowly your sense of self gets eroded until you become nothing but a puppet who fulfills the narcissist's needs. Therefore, it is crucial to confront abuse. This doesn't be fighting tooth and nail with the narcissist for every single thing. Instead, it means standing your ground, speaking up for yourself, and setting boundaries that protect your sense of self and character. You are entitled to be treated with respect, but respect isn't given freely. It has to be earned. Thus, you should set boundaries in your relationship, and when those boundaries get pushed or broken, you should take immediate action.

Immediate action doesn't mean that you should immediately leave your partner forever. Instead, it means that you reinforce your boundaries, stress what would happen if they get broken again, and if they do get broken, only then should you take severe action. You should state to the narcissist in straight and concise words about your wishes so that they can understand your position and don't try to get back into your good graces.

2. Timeout

If you've realized that your partner has been abusing you for years, but you don't wish to leave them forever or break ties with them, perhaps they are a family member or a close friend, then you should walk away from them for a while to compile all your thoughts and feelings to make a decision. In this time, you should also educate yourself about the manipulative tendencies displayed by the narcissist and take a long and hard look at their behavior over the past few years.

If they are receptive, talk to them about their behavior and tell them that you have some boundaries that should never be crossed again, and if they ever are, then you will walk away from them. However, they may try to manipulate you emotionally, decrying your actions and waling at the unfairness of it all. Therefore, stay vigilant when enforcing your boundaries. But remember that this timeout is for your peace of mind, not the narcissists, and should, therefore, be taken as such.

3. Low Contact

The effects of abuse can be debilitating on some people, and constant contact with the abuser can increase these effects, including flashbacks, panic attacks, nightmares, and difficulty in emotional regulation. A victim who is constantly exposed to their abuser may end up even more traumatized, and this constant exposure can, over time, can drastically change the personality or self of the victim due to the adverse effects on several regions of the brain. Thus, constant and prolonged abuse is extremely bad for the continued well-being of the victim.

Also, abuse is something that should never do done to anyone. Everybody should be treated with respect. Therefore, if you think that staying with your partner does more harm than good, by all means, limit contact with them or walk away from them if you so, please. If for some reason, you cannot limit contact with them or can't cut them off entirely, maybe because they're an acquaintance, a friend, or someone close to you, then you should minimize contact with them as much as you can. Not only will this low contact save you from manipulation, but it will also grant you peace of mind. You may interact with the narcissist and be cordial with them on many occasions, but you won't be in their vicinity. It would be best if you strived not to answer any of their personal questions to ward off any blackmail or humiliation and be vigilant of their manipulations.

4. Grey Rock

Say you have children together with the narcissist or have ties to the narcissist that don't allow you to walk away from them, then limiting all contact is not an option. The grey rock method, in this case, can be beneficial because it only allows the necessary communication that is needed. You aren't involved with your partner at all. You have to do some small talk (providing the narcissist with the barest minimum information about yourself).

This method can be used when the narcissist is usually someone who works, lives, or is near you at all times. The only way to keep yourself going is to ignore the narcissist's manipulations, set boundaries, and keep them away from important information that could be, in their hands, very dangerous. Eventually, the narcissist may get bored with your refusal to pay them any attention and may move on.

5. Changing the Subject

If discussion of the narcissist causes you pain or drives you to anxiety, you should avoid talking about them. If somebody starts talking about them, and you feel incredibly panicky and fearful, you should change the subject for your peace of mind. However, clamming up entirely can be harmful to your health. If the symptoms of your depression are very debilitating, you should seek the help of a therapist or a psychiatrist and talk to them about what you've been through. These professionals know what to say and do for you and can help you start your journey to healing.

But, if you're still in a relationship with a narcissist, and you know that they're going to explode if you raise a particular issue, you should then change the subject or not talk about the issue at all because you know the consequences of your actions. However, keep in mind that relationships should never be based on lies. If you find some aspect of your partner's character or personality a bit uneasy, you should observe them first and then tell them about what worries you. Their reaction will be your answer as to whether you should stay with them or not.

6. Manage Expectations

Most of the time, we get hurt by other people because we expect too much. We expect people to be kind in turn when we are kind to them. We expect them to help when we help them, and we expect them to be cordial when we are cordial to them. The problem with the narcissist is that they don't care to reciprocate anything. They have no desire to meet or manage your wants and needs because of their extreme selfishness. Therefore, manage your expectations around the narcissist. Don't hope for things from them that you expect from everybody else. Be cautious and vigilant because narcissistic are incredible manipulators who make people dance to their tune through their charm and charisma.

However, this doesn't mean that you accept their abuse or excuse their behavior. Instead, it means that you pay attention to the narcissist's behavior and modus operandi and try to limit yourself from depending on them.

7. Set and Maintain Boundaries

Another way you can manage narcissistic abuse is by setting concrete boundaries. Nobody is going you protect your other than yourself. In other words, you are your best protector. Establishing boundaries is what keeps the wheels of society running. Laws exist for the survival of civilization, moral rules are there to maintain peace in our natures, and societal rules enforce that no one appreciates certain behaviors. Unfortunately, narcissists do not pander to these rules. Therefore, they believe in their superiority and think that no law applies to them. For many people with high-spectrum NPD, might is right. If they can take it, it is theirs. Therefore, if you don't want to lose yourself to the narcissist, you should strive to set down boundaries that limit their jurisdiction over you and your sense of self.

When you set a boundary, always ensure that there are consequences attached to its breaking. If the narcissist doesn't understand this or thinks that they will get away with breaking these boundaries, make it clear that this is not so, that there will be consequences for their actions, only then can you live peacefully with a narcissist. The narcissist will constantly test your resilience and your will to maintain the boundary, so you should strive to remain strong and face them head-on when they try to violate your boundaries.

8. Depersonalize

Being in a relationship and receiving harsh words for your efforts can be the most demoralizing of hurts. Someone in a relationship with a narcissist should remember that their partner doesn't care for them. Foremost in the narcissist mind is himself—he only cares for his needs and wants and projects them on you. He thinks you're subservient to him—second to him—and are not worth pining over or pandering to.

Therefore, never take the narcissist's harsh comments to heart. They are speaking out of their own affronted arrogance. They want to demoralize you to become more malleable in their hands. They want you to become their pawn. Narcissists do not care for your wishes; they care for their own, and it is this egotistic nature combined with a perfectionistic personality with low self-esteem that makes them highly volatile.

Thus, try to distance yourself from the narcissist and their antics and try not to take everything too personally. When you react emotionally, you only play into the narcissist's hands.

9. Resist Arguments

As mentioned before, arguing with a narcissist does nothing but bring you misery. When you try to explain yourself or say to them about their behavior, the narcissist may lash out at you, causing you pain. Narcissists, as a rule, are self-absorbed, which is why explaining why you were hurt means nothing to them.

Another problem created by arguments is the rage created in the narcissist's heart. Narcissists, by nature, are perfectionists. They believe they can't do any wrong, which is why when you point out their faults to their face, they become violent and unpredictable.

Therefore, try to avoid arguments as much as you can with the narcissist because they will not listen to you no matter how right you are. They will try to impose their will onto you, and when you disapprove of it, they will become wrathful and take out their anger on you.

However, it is best kept in mind that bowing down to the verbally abusive, manipulative, or exploitative tactics used by a narcissist do not make a relationship better. Instead, if you walk away from arguments all the time, the narcissist may start to perceive you as someone who is weak and may, in time, become more abusive toward you. So, use this diversion tactic for small arguments or disagreements, but try not to use it every time you talk to the narcissist. Show your backbone and set boundaries. Only then will you be able to stop the narcissist from walking all over you.

WORK ON YOUR PERSONAL HEALING

1. If you broke free, think of yourself as a hero

Anyone who has the willpower to break free from an abusive narcissistic relationship should be congratulated for their achievement. Often, people who live with narcissistic partners are unaware of the true nature of their partner. They may think that their partner is sweet when they are cutting, helpful when they are sarcastic, kind when they've been manipulative, and charming when exploitative. It takes incredible willpower to see through this veneer, and it takes even more resolves to break free from the cage the narcissist has strung around you.

2. Do a full medical check

The moment you get out from under the thumb of the narcissist, go to a medical professional and get a checkup. Constant stress can have adverse effects on your body. Cortisol, the stress hormone produce during stressful situations, is terrible for mental health. In various scientific researches, it has been found that this hormone changes the size of some specific regions of the brain, causing short-term memory loss and making a person more emotional. Checking the levels of this hormone, along with other bloodwork and relevant work, can help you discover if you have any latent problems caused by the stress you had borne under the narcissist's ministrations.

3. Arm yourself with understanding

Education is the key to understanding. It can clarify things you had previously only an inkling or instinct. To save yourself from falling into the nets of other narcissists, learn everything you can about them. Research about narcissistic personality disorder, read self-help books and scientific literature to inform yourself about the qualities exhibited by people with narcissistic tendencies.

Read up to arm yourself with weapons to protect yourself, and don't shy away from the truth; after all, the fact will only hurt you once, but lies will come back to haunt you forever. Therefore, learn as much as you can about narcissists to understand what makes them tick and how you can identify them so you don't fall into their charismatic, kindly, and loving trap again.

4. Deal with the mental issues the relationship left you with

Living with a narcissist can change your sense of self and your perception. People who survive the abuse perpetrated by such people often have short-term and long-term effects on their mental well-being. Narcissists destroy their victim's self-worth, sense of self, personality, values, and boundaries.

The body internalizes and reacts to the stress caused by this abuse in many ways. People who have been through this kind of abuse often complain about feeling stressed, on edge, tired, and ill. They may display cognitive and mental effects of the abuse, such as nightmares, hypervigilance, suspiciousness, intrusive thoughts, heightened or lowered level of alertness, poor short-term memory and concentration, and constant confusion. They may also display behavioral issues such as a change in communication, antisocial acts, withdrawal from daily life, inability to relax, loss or increase of appetite, and reduced social mobility. The most common of these effects are anxiety and fear, which leads to depression.

Recovering from such an ordeal isn't easy. The victim has to work very hard to recover what they lost. They lived with the narcissist, and this recovery takes a lot of time. Consider the example of an extensive program or file. It takes time to transfer that program or file to another area. Similarly, it takes time for the victim to carve new neural pathways through their brain to help them live life as they want to.

Something all victims should do is to seek professional help. Medical professionals such as psychiatrists, therapists, and counselors are trained to help abuse victims through their recovery process. They use techniques that can calm your fear and anxiety and can suggest techniques that you can participate in or use to recover from your ordeal. The most used therapies or techniques recommended by medical professionals for narcissistic abuse victims are cognitive behavioral therapy and group therapy, both of which have been discussed in chapter 1.

5. Work on regaining your self-worth and positive perspective to yourself and your relationships with others

Abuse is both emotionally, behaviorally, and psychologically taxing. It damages the psyche of the person who undergoes it. In the case of narcissistic abuse, the effects of the trauma are usually incredibly damaging. They can leave the victim feeling depressed, anxious, fearful, and emotionally volatile. The victim may feel that they don't deserve anything in the world, that they are worthless, and that their opinions don't matter. This kind of thinking can be highly debilitating and can hold back those victims from progressing wholeheartedly into their recovery.

The victims may even start to believe that they are not worth anything and may sink into a deep and unhealthy depression as a result.

To counter this effect of abuse, victims should seek help from medical professionals such as therapists, counselors, and psychiatrists. They should also seek help from their family, friends, and colleagues and focus on themselves first and foremost. Victims should remember that they are not worthless, that their life has meaning, and that many people love them unconditionally.

6. You should work on your desire to want to change for the best

Nobody can force anyone to do anything. They can manipulate and exploit them into doing something, but the final responsibility of the act resides with the one who did the action. Of course, there are extenuating circumstances, such as abuse, trauma, and self-defense, but in this case of recovery, the final say and choice reside with the victim. If you think that you are worthless and can't do anything right, then you may find yourself in a state of fugue, without being able to do anything. This means that if you think negatively that you can't recover, you will not recover because you aren't putting all the effort into doing so.

Therefore, to recover from narcissistic abuse, try to put in the effort and change your perspective. Believing there is nothing for you in life will only make your recovery stagnant, but believing that you are worthy of a better life can be the instigating factor to recovery. Try to put the abuse in the past and focus on the future. Remaining in the past will bring you nothing except misery. You will always be thinking about what-ifs and how you could've done something else to stop the mistake before it happened.

7. Create a support system

No man is an island. We all depend on others to fulfill our emotional and physical needs. Humans are social creatures, and we need social interactions to feel normal—to have a support network that can help in times of hardship. The narcissist, in the relationship, tries to do the opposite. They cut their victim off from everybody and make sure that he/she is only dependent on them. They don't want their victim to tell others what is happening to him/her, so they cut he/she off from family and friends. This can lead to incredible loneliness on the victim's part—they become isolated.

The consequence of this isolation is that when the victim finally breaks free of the narcissist's cage, they realize that they have no one left to help them because the narcissist made them push everyone away. They may try to recover from the abuse they suffered in attempting to do everything themselves, but usually, this is a losing proposition. Which is why, instead of isolating yourself because you are too embarrassed or mortified to go back to your loved ones, try to set aside your pride and go to them. Revive your friendship and your family bonds. Tell them what you suffered through and why you had to do as you did. Accept responsibility for your actions, not the narcissists, and tell the tale like it is. The support you get from your friends and family can be an incredible help. They can guide you to better professionals, can support you when you're down, and can take care of you when you aren't in a state to do it for yourself. They can also love you unconditionally when you seem to be incapable of loving yourself. Therefore, don't isolate yourself and try to reopen your battered heart to those who were once close to you. You will find ease in them.

8. Distance yourself from the source of the abuse

Healing in a stressful environment is almost impossible for anybody. Just like constant exertion is terrible for someone with a torn tendon, constant exposure to the narcissist is bad for the victim. Whenever the victim is faced with the narcissist, they may remember the things the narcissist said or did to them—the hurts and wounds they gave them. No matter at which stage of healing they may be, the victim may feel bruised by just an encounter with the narcissist. They may start dwelling on the relationship, ponder what happened to them and become emotionally volatile when they remember what happened to them, sabotaging all the progress they made in the healing process.

This is why the victim, when they get out of the relationship, should try their hardest to walk away from thoughts of the narcissist. They should focus on themselves and their recovery and shouldn't focus on what-ifs and what-could-be-s because nothing hurts a victim as much as their inability to do anything.

Therefore, a victim should stay away from the narcissist and avoid thinking about them to speed up their healing. The benefit of this constant ignorance would be that the victim will find themselves more emotionally stable and may, in time, recover much of what they lost to the narcissist—foremost of which is their sense of self and independence.

9. Work on your boundaries

Most of the time, we incur sorrow from the actions of others because we do not enforce our will enough on subjects that are important to us. In the case of a narcissistic relationship, the victim constantly bows to the narcissist's demands to either stop the narcissist from lashing out at them, run with what they know, or save themselves from unnecessary fights. Seeing this submissive attitude, the narcissist may capitalize on your lack of sufficient boundaries and manipulate you into doing things you would never have thought to do in the first place.

This is why it is imperative to enforce your boundaries at every stage of your relationship. If you don't want to do something, tell your partner precisely that. If you think that something is atrocious or not to your liking, tell them that too. Only you can save yourself from doing things you don't want to do, and you can't do it if you're laid-back and allow people to walk all over you.

10. Think about what is really important in your life

What do you think is the most critical thing in your life? What do you think matters most to you? Find the answers to these questions. Going to life adrift without any purpose can become tiring over time. A purposeless individual is liable to get manipulated by others very quickly because, for a time, they find meaning in someone else's purpose. They may put all their effort into doing things for the other person, only to be left behind when that person is done with them. That is essentially what narcissists do to their victims in a relationship. They take everything their victim gives them and give nothing back in return.

Therefore, unless you want to continue this pattern of giving everything and getting nothing back, you should try to think about what is most important to you in your life. Your first answer should be yourself. If you aren't there anymore, what is the point of life? Focus on the positive aspects of your life, live a little, forget the hurts that people caused you, learn from your mistakes, and move on from the troubles that plague you. Find what you love most in life and embrace life—for it is, after all, a challenge worthy of taking.

11. Look for assistive therapies

Along with medical therapy that helps victims recover from their trauma with the help of another person, there is also assistive therapy that can help them deal with the pain of the trauma by themselves. Assistive treatment can come in various forms, such as meditation, yoga, mindfulness, and relaxing Pilates sessions. This therapy aims to make the person who does it calm enough to help them go through their worries and thoughts.

12. Connect to your old interests or find new ones

Many times, revamping what you love can help you assume control of your life, but at other times, finding new interests can prove to be even more therapeutic. Every experience in our life changes us. Every fresh wound, hurt, or action we commit transforms us into something new. We learn from everything that we do. In the aftermath of a narcissistic relationship, a person realizes that they may have lost sight of themselves in the constant abuse they suffered. They realize that they have lost a piece of themselves.

So, to recover this lost piece of yourself, try to recultivate your old interests. If you loved to dress up in fancy clothes, by all means, do it. If you loved to paint, try to reconnect to it again. Dust off the hobbies that you had abandoned and try to find yourself in them. If you instead find that you have changed too much due to the new experiences you've had: don't worry.

Instead of recultivating your old loves, discover new things to love. Talk to people, take art classes or martial art classes, if you will. Do yoga. Try everything to find something you love.

You may not succeed on your first try or tenth but in all your experimentation. You may find yourself the beneficiary of some lovely skills that would help you later in life. The bonus of this experimentation: you may recover the parts of your sense of self that you think you lost in the trauma and bolster your self-esteem in the process.

13. Fall in love with yourself

You are the only one present on the Earth who knows yourself as fully as possible. You have been there for yourself at your best and worst. You have seen yourself do the worst and the best, and you have had a front-row seat to everything that has happened in your life. You know every aspect of yourself. You know your mistakes and why you made those mistakes, and you know how strong you are. This means that you are the only one who sees and will see the true potential and range of your strengths and weaknesses. You are the only one capable of loving yourself as fully as possible. When you love yourself, you acknowledge your faults and strengths, and you learn to recognize other people's faults and strengths without casting judgment.

Remember that the whorls in your thumbprint are the only ones in existence. This means that there is only one of your kind in existence. Thus, appreciate your uniqueness and revel in the fact that there is no one else like you on Earth. Learn from your mistakes—because you will make many—and put the lessons you learn from them to work. Improve yourself constantly because life is not stagnant—it is fluid forever.

6

10 STEPS TO RECOVERY

Narcissistic abuse is hard to overcome, but just because something is hard doesn't mean that it is impossible. This kind of abuse destroys a person's sense of self, security, and stability and makes them emotionally volatile. Therefore, breaking free of this abuse is a tricky thing to do, but accepting the impact the abuse had on you can be even more challenging.

Trauma acts as a catalyst for us to better engage in self-care and introduces us to endless modalities for healing and expressing ourselves, and helps us turn our crisis into our transformation. To do this, all you require is resilience, love, and compassion for yourself, understanding, and the will to do what needs to be done.

The first step into healing from narcissistic abuse is to stop the confusion and mistrust of yourself the narcissist has led you into. You have to recover your sense of self and trust in yourself, both of which you can do by following these 3 steps.

RECOVERY STEP 1: NAME THINGS FOR WHAT THEY ARE

Healing is a convoluted journey—it is a complex and multifaceted process that includes ups and downs, breakdowns and breakthroughs, and love and hate. Sometimes you may be walking on thorns through the journey, and other times you're maybe running like there is no tomorrow. Some days just getting out of bed may be the hardest thing you do, and on other days you may find yourself walking firmly—without any misstep towards your goal. Like a caterpillar that turns into a butterfly—you also change, shatter, explode, and are reborn into a new person.

This change process is painful, cruel, horrific, imperfect, and messy, but it can also be beautiful, life-changing, inspiring, and extraordinary. It brings you joy and pain in equal measures. To initiate this process of healing, you can't hide from it. You can't sweep your pain under the rug and hold your breath in the hope that it will go away. You can't seek professional help or invalidate your experience because you feel like it. If you wish to heal your wounds, you, instead, have to look at what happened to you directly, face it, and come out the better person on the other end.

People often forget what the narcissist did to them after they separate from them. Don't make this mistake. The narcissist abused you—don't invalidate their actions. Do not forget the hurt they caused you nor the manipulations they did to elicit specific responses from you because if you do, you may let the narcissist into your life again. Therefore, understand that the narcissist meant to do the things he did to you. Nothing happened to you spontaneously or erroneously—every traumatic moment was deliberate and delivered with the maximum impact.

But, in the pursuit of this understanding—for seeing things as they are, don't forget to accept your emotions and the fact that what you went through was traumatic. Remember that your abuser is still an abuser and that you do not excuse their actions. Don't try to repress your emotions or prevent yourself from getting help because such blockages can hinder your healing. Allow yourself to cry when you need to and laugh when you need to. Don't try to bypass negative emotions to be positive. You need to process and work through your more complex emotions, so looking away from them won't help. Be truthful to both yourself and others.

RECOVERY STEP 2: PUTTING THE RELATIONSHIP IN PERSPECTIVE: UNCOVER THE LIES

Narcissists are compulsive liars because they want to be seen as the best at everything. This is why they embroider their achievements or lack of accomplishments, augment their life story to make it more sympathy-inducing, and lie about everything they can get away with. This lying is what pains the abuse survivor the most. They don't know what was real and what wasn't. They may not even know the true story of the narcissist, lies that they carefully cultivated to gain sympathy.

As mentioned in the previous step, once you become aware of the reality of the situation, you have to deal with it. In this step, you have to take things a bit further. You have to start analyzing the relationship and weed out the lies the narcissist told you from the truth of their words and actions. Because when you're in pain, you try to find excuses for the narcissist's actions. But that's not what you need to do here. You have to focus on the truth of the situation and realize that all the things the narcissist may have told you might not be true, that whatever they did for you had an ulterior motive, and that motive is something that you have to analyze yourself.

RECOVERY STEP 3: FIND THE TRUTH

Narcissists are brilliant at manipulating and exploiting their victims, especially narcissists with a high-spectrum narcissistic personality disorder. They bombard you with love, attention, and interest at the start of the relationship to lull you into a false sense of security. They then collect information about you—what makes you tick—and then use this information to get the response from you that they desire. This constant manipulation when you look back renders some of the most tender and beautiful moments you had with the narcissist complete and utter lies. You may even see those events with a completely different perspective once you realize the truth about your partner. There is a difference between honesty and truth. Honesty can be subjective, but the truth is always objective. You may want to believe what you think happened, but the truth may be something else entirely—this gulf between what you think and what can be very wide.

You may want to think that his endearing words and actions were actual, but the way he treated you at the end of the relationship says otherwise. The promises he made you when you started dating that he broke at the end. The love that he promised turned to hate. All of the little things for which you stayed with him may as well have been a lie. Therefore, in this step, focus on the reality of the situation. Take a clear look at the things that do not make logical sense, such as unexplained absences, illogical excuses, blatant lies, and dissonant actions—

where the words say something else. In contrast, body language still says other things. Look closely at the daily minutiae of your relationship with him and find out what was the truth or not. Realizing that whatever he said to you

was not the fact that will make the recovery process that much easier for you.

Next, you will need to work through your pain—both the pain you experienced in the cycle of abuse and the pain you are experiencing as a lasting effect of your relationship even after a breakup. This is the pain you tried to uncover in the 3 previous steps. The following 4 steps will help you through it.

RECOVERY STEP 4: KNOW THAT IT'S NOT YOUR FAULT

Before you start finding ways to treat the pain, you have to first look at why you are in so much pain in the first place. Narcissists mold their victims into the shape they want. They do this with careful and subtle manipulation, brain-washing/gaslighting, and exploitation. Every single utterance with exactness is calculated to get the effect they want. Once a whole person with a structured sense of self at the beginning of the relationship, you become a collection of fragments near the end of the relationship. Your instincts start warring with the instincts the narcissist instilled in you. You may conclude that everything wrong that happened to you was your fault. Your fault that you like things the narcissist didn't like. Your fault that everything you created was atrocious and bland, and your fault that you were too pretty, too intelligent, or just too much.

Getting out of a relationship when you've become subservient to your partner is one of the hardest things to do. The narcissist tries to make everything your fault. He blames the way the relationship collapsed on you. He places the blame for all the things that went wrong at your feet and tried his hardest to make you believe it wholeheartedly. You, broken and feeling worthless at this point, believe him because you trust him to do best for you. What you don't know is that he doesn't want to do his best for you. He wants everything for himself. He thinks that all the admiration, adoration, and attention should be his. That he is worthy of the best, and you aren't.

When you get out of the relationship, you may think that everything is your fault. But after inspecting the relationship for what it is, you start to see the holes in the tales the narcissist weaved for you. You see the lies for what they are, and they manipulate trickery. When you do this and see the reality of the situation, remember that what happened to you was not your fault. The narcissist deliberately targeted you because you had one of those too many qualities (too lovely, too famous, too beautiful, too kind, etc.). He wanted the admiration you had from other people for himself. He wanted you, a vaunted individual, to bow before him, to profess.his superiority over him, and you did.

Therefore, never put yourself at blame unnecessarily, instead blame the narcissist for his actions, the manipulations that he did deliberately, the lies he told without remorse, and the hurt he caused you without thinking about it. It is all his fault. You have to remember that.

RECOVERY STEP 5: WORK THROUGH THE PAIN

Narcissists are attention-seeking and self-centered individuals. They work for their best interests and don't care about how they achieve and get what they want. They will lie, cheat, manipulate, exploit, and brainwash their victim to get what they want. A narcissist cares nothing for your emotions, needs, or desires. To them, their needs and wants triumph over yours. They trod all over you and railroad you into doing the things they want. They do not care what happens to you in the process.

They may use the silent treatment as a way to torment their partner. The purpose of the silent treatment may be to elicit a particular reaction, such as fear, anxiety, depression, nostalgia, terror, pain, and more. The silence, at specific moments, may be deafening, a bottomless void that goes on forever. You may feel that you have been abandoned, left for the crows, until just as you're about to fade into the woodwork of your life, the narcissist appears, like a clown out of a box, back into your life.

Dealing with this treatment can be particularly hard. You may be worried and terrified of the narcissist. You may leave a message on their phone and email with their acquaintances, family, friends, and workers. You may become so worried the first time this happens to you that you may cause yourself physical harm. The narcissist, of course, wants this reaction. They want you to pine after them, to remember and miss them. They want all your attention, and they will do anything to get it. The silent treatment is one excruciating way to do this.

To work through the pain caused by this discard-and-take-back-again process, you have to find in yourself the ability to appreciate the silence caused by the absence of the narcissist. Instead of feeling abandoned by the narcissist, try to remain positive. You only feel abandoned by him because you become a part of him now. You can think of yourself as separate from him. Lead this way of thinking behind. You are your person. You can find someone to compliment you, but you do not need them to make you whole. Therefore, separate yourself from the narcissist; realize that their needs are not your needs; you are not their servant, nor should you be; you are their partner, and if they don't treat you as one, then you shouldn't be with them in the first place.

RECOVERY STEP 6: DISCOVER YOUR BOUNDARIES

All of us have unestablished and un-concrete boundaries. We know instinctively when we do or do not appreciate something. Boundaries are based on our moral principles, which can stem from our deepest feelings about something, such as torture, and our beliefs, such as being kind to others. Most of the time, we are unaware of these boundaries and don't know what they are. But when someone breaks them, we finally realize that they do exist and that their breakage hurts.

Narcissists break the boundaries of their victim's multitudes of times. They may lie to their partner, knowing that their partner doesn't condone lying. They manipulate and exploit their partner and can even have them cross the moral boundaries they hold dear. They find out what values their partner holds dear. Instead, their partner surrenders the information to them, willingly assured in the knowledge that they will not be harmed by those who profess to love them. The narcissist then weaponizes this information and trespasses the boundaries of their victims hundreds of times to get what they want. To very high-spectrum narcissists, no boundary is off-limits. If you were abused sometime in your life, they would remind you of that abuse to objectify you and make you feel horrible about yourself. If something worse happened to you before you met the narcissist, they would use that knowledge to torture you into doing what they want. When a narcissist pursues what they want, they have no mercy for their victims. They trod over them, uncaring of the damage they instill.

If you're unaware of your boundaries, you can use the pain caused by the narcissist's antics to realize where they are. If you felt incredibly betrayed when the narcissist lied to you, chances are you hold the value that lying to those you lose is terrible. If you were horrified by the casual disdain, the narcissist showed to people, and you might hold the boundary of being unfailingly kind towards others. By analyzing the origin of the pain you bear, you can identify your limitations. Once you figure them out, you will know when someone breaks them and realize who to avoid and who not to.

RECOVERY STEP 7: FIND CLOSURE AND MOVE ON

Closure, nowadays, means that something is wrapped in a lovely tiny bow with no messy wrapping or any feeling leaking out. In simpler words, it is regarded as the fairytale happily ever after where the end is lovely, beautiful, and amiable. However, real-life doesn't work that way. When something ends or is lost, we cry, bawl, and howl in agony, fear, or incredible pain. Asking for a pretty, emotionless end is like asking for the moon. You just can't get it. All of us are human, and we are invested in the relationships we hold dear. So, asking for closure—when it means a HEA—is futile and a waste of time, especially for a trauma survivor. After all, how could the narcissist provide you with relief when he has tortured you throughout the relationship? What do you think the narcissist will offer to you? They manipulated you, cheated on you, lied to you, exploited you, and brainwashed you into doing the things they wanted you to do. How do you expect them to put your best interests forward when they've never paid them any attention to your relationship?

This leaves you only one option: you have to make your closure. You have to make your own happy ending, and you can't create that without letting what the narcissist did to you go. It would be best if you focused more on yourself and your well-being rather than focusing on someone who did excessive harm to you in the first place.

You cannot heal if you keep dwelling on your relationship with the narcissist. After you've worked to break the vicious cycle they led you into, it is time to work on moving on. Steps 8 to 10 will help you do just that.

RECOVERY STEP 8: FACE YOUR FEARS

Most of the time, we stay in a relationship with a narcissist because we are afraid of change. We are so scared that leaving the narcissist will leave us alone and empty, that nobody will love us more than the narcissist will, or that the narcissist will hurt us if we leave them. A mother might remain with her narcissistic husband for the sake of her children. A girlfriend may stay with her narcissistic boyfriend because she doesn't feel as loved by anyone as she does by her boyfriend. A nephew may maintain his relationship with his narcissistic uncle because he owes the uncle a debt. The reasons for staying with someone who abuses you are varied and many, but one of the main reasons is vulnerability.

People try to stay and stick with the familiar because they feel vulnerable otherwise. They may be afraid of change or just the unknown. They condone abuse, year after year because the alternative is worse. They fear the unknown more than they fear their abuser. After all, the enemy you know is better than the one you don't know. In this case, your enemy is your vulnerability. You are scared of being alone, of being unappreciated, of facing reality... the reasons are endless. The narcissist finds out these reasons, and then he exploits you through your vulnerabilities. If you fear pain, he will threaten you with pain if you don't do something for them. If you're afraid of falling in love, they may capitalize on that fear and saturate you with it. The scent your fear like a shark and then stalk you to the cliff until you fall off, never to return to who you once were.

The only way to get out of this cycle is to start facing your fears. If you fear rejection or loneliness, remember that not everybody will like you for who you are. Just like you have different tastes, so do other people. Asking everybody to appreciate you for who you are is a wasting proposition. You will get nothing out of it. Meet your fears head on to reduce your dependability on the narcissist and to seek out another life—one that is wholly your own.

RECOVERY STEP 9: DECIDE WHAT YOU WANT IN LIFE

Going through life as a boat cut adrift—purposeless—avails you nothing but misery. Narcissists will target you because you seem vulnerable and need direction. Multitudes of people will benefit from your abilities because you can't seem to have a path to follow in life. All of this give-give-give attitude will only make you more miserable. You will give your all to other people, but other people will never give you anything in return. They will capitalize on your efforts and will never appreciate you.

Knowing what you want beforehand can be both a blessing and a curse. The benefits of nothing that you wish to are varied and many. For example, you can set boundaries that you weren't able to do before. You may be less vulnerable and prone to manipulation, more energetic, better informed, and more logical. You may even be able to identify when others try to manipulate you into doing things for them. You may have an established list of qualities you look for in your partner or significant other. In other words, by knowing what you want, you can develop boundaries and values for yourself. If you want kindness, then you can talk to kind people. If you want appreciation, then you can work towards that goal. If you hate lying, then you can stress to both yourself and other people that you despise it.

Being aware of your needs and wants can help you decide the path you want to lead in life and can make it harder for you to be caught in the trap laid by a narcissist.

RECOVERY STEP 10: BECOME INDEPENDENT: HOPE FOR YOURSELF

All a narcissist wants from you is that you give them all your attention, admiration, and affection. They want everything that you have used for their gain, not yours, theirs. They don't care about you as a person and do not consider your needs at all. They think they deserve the best, and they will do anything to get that perceived best. Narcissists start the relationships by bombing you with appreciation, affection, and admiration. They put you on a pedestal and marvel at your achievement until you become dependent on their praise and love. Then they start exploiting you to do what they want.

This tendency to depend on the narcissist lands most victims in trouble. When the narcissist turns into a jerk, they still hope for that long-lost love. When they suffer cruelty at the narcissist's hands, they condone it and try to explain it away because they love him. They increase their efforts to make sure that the narcissist never feels abandoned. They think: maybe if I gave him everything he will love me. But this is not what happens.

The narcissist takes, but he doesn't give back anything. He never appreciates your sacrifice and doesn't acknowledge the hardship you may go through to give them what they want. You hope and hope and provide them with everything in the process, but you never get the love you want because they are incapable of giving it.

This is why it is better to stop depending on the narcissist. It is better for your well-being that instead of linking all your needs and wants with their needs and wants, you should try to become your own person. Instead of seeking validation from them for everything you do, you should try to build yourself up. Make your world revolve around yourself rather than someone who despises you and treats you with contempt. Love yourself and appreciate yourself, and don't surrender yourself to someone who doesn't even respect you—who will never appreciate you.

CONCLUSION

Narcissistic abuse is insidious, subtle, and manipulative. Narcissists themselves are cunning, attention-seeking, self-centered, admiration-seeking. They think the world of themselves and deserve the best things regardless of ability or accomplishment. They want to be the best at everything, which is why they chase perfection and believe that they can create something perfect. Their arrogance is such that they disregard the opinions of people who are more educated, more brilliant, and more intelligent than them.

When narcissists get into a relationship with someone, they smother him/her. They project their own needs over the needs of their victim and try their hardest to make their victim dependent on them for appreciation, affection, and love. They exploit, brainwash, and manipulate their victim into doing the things they want them to do. They hunt aggressively for the vulnerabilities of their selected prey and then use those vulnerabilities to force their partner to do what they want. They abuse their partners.

This constant abuse can traumatize the victim. The victim slowly loses their sense of self and self-esteem and becomes doubtful of everything they do. They become emotionally volatile, full of fear and anxiety, and a shadow of themselves. They may suffer from nightmares and flashbacks of the abuse they suffered and may not be able to, for a time, move into society. Getting out of this trauma is one of the hardest things a victim could do. Some victims may not even have the willpower to force themselves to confront their partner's lies and truths. But, if they do this, they may find themselves all the wiser than they used to be. Their transformation will be messy, cruel, and painful, but in the end, they will emerge a better, more beautiful, and lovelier person than they ever were. All it takes is strength and the will to do what needs to be done.

Thank you for reading Narcissistic Abuse and Trauma. Thank you for spending this time with me and allowing me to show you the truth about narcissistic abuse. I hope you will return to the book as needed, and each time you do, my prayer for you is that a new sweetness enriches your recovery. Always remember that being a target of psychological abuse was not your fault. You did not attract abuse into your life, nor did you force someone to abuse you. You never asked for or wanted what was done to you. Now is your time to take what you have learned, process it, and then implement it on yourself and others around you. You can use the knowledge you now possess deep within you to help other people going through narcissistic abuse and yourself.

If you liked this book, please consider leaving a review on Amazon. Every review helps spread out the word about this book to those who desperately need it. Thank you for being with me on this journey. I wish you the best of luck! Remember, **This is a Marathon not a Sprint.**

LEAVE A 1-CLICK REVIEW!!!!

I would be incredibly thankful if you could take 60 seconds to write a brief review on Amazon, even if it is just a few sentences!

REFERENCES

American Psychiatric Association's (2013) Diagnostic and Statistical Manual of Mental Disorders (5th ed.; DSM-5).

Nikhil Dhawan, Mark E. Kunik, John Oldham, John Coverdale, *Prevalence and treatment of narcissistic personality disorder in the community: a systematic review*, Comprehensive Psychiatry, Volume 51, Issue 4, 2010, Pages 333-339, ISSN 0010-440X, https://doi.org/10.1016/j.comppsych.2009.09.003.

Sigmund Karterud, Maria Øien, Geir Pedersen, *Validity aspects of the Diagnostic and Statistical Manual of Mental Disorders, Fourth Edition, narcissistic personality disorder construct, Comprehensive Psychiatry*, Volume 52, Issue 5, 2011, Pages 517-526, ISSN 0010-440X, https://doi.org/10.1016/j.comppsych.2010.11.001.

Torgerson, Epidemiology. Oldham JM, Skodol AE, Dender DS. *The American Psychiatric Publishing Textbook of Personality Disorders.* Washington, DC: American Psychiatric Publishing; 2005. 129-141

Ronningstam E. *Narcissistic Personality Disorder: Facing DSM-V. Psychiatric Annals.* 2009 Mar. 39: 111-121.

Stinson, F. S., Dawson, D. A., Goldstein, R. B., Chou, S. P., Huang, B., Smith, S. M., Ruan, W. J., Pulay, A. J., Saha, T. D., Pickering, R. P., & Grant, B. F. *Prevalence, correlates, disability, and comorbidity of DSM-IV narcissistic personality disorder: results from the wave 2 national epidemiologic survey on alcohol and related conditions.* The Journal of clinical psychiatry, 69(7), (2008), 1033–1045. https://doi.org/10.4088/jcp.v69n0701

American Psychiatric Association. *Alternative DSM-5 model for personality disorders.* Fifth Edition. Washington, DC: American Psychiatric Publishing, Inc; 2013. 761—81

Eve Caligor, M.D., Kenneth N. Levy., Ph.D., Frank E. Yeomans, M.D., Ph.D. *Narcissistic Personality Disorder: Diagnostic and Clinical Challenges.* The American Journal of Psychiatry, Volume 172, Issue 5, 2015, 415-422. https://doi.org/10.1176/appi.ajp.2014.14060723

Roth BE. Narcissistic patients in group therapy: containing affects in the early group. Ronningstam E. *Disorders of Narcis-*

sism: Diagnostic, Clinical, and Empirical Implications. Washington DC: American Psychiatric Press; 1998. 221-238.

Ronningstam EF, Maltsberger JT. Part X: Personality Disorders. Gabbard GO. Gabbard's Treatments of Psychiatric Disorders. Fourth Edition. Washington Dc: American Psychiatric Publishing; 2007. Chapter 52: Narcissistic Personality Disorder, pages 791-804.

Alonso A. The shattered mirror: treatment of a group of narcissistic patients. Group. 1992. 16: 210-219.

Carter, G. L., & Douglass, M. D. (2018). The Aging Narcissus: Just a Myth? Narcissism Moderates the Age-Loneliness Relationship in Older Age. Frontiers in psychology, 9, 1254. https://doi.org/10.3389/fpsyg.2018.01254

www.ingramcontent.com/pod-product-compliance
Lightning Source LLC
Chambersburg PA
CBHW070043120526
44589CB00035B/2268